*OTHER BOOKS BY GREVILLE JANNER
INCLUDE*

JANNER'S EMPLOYMENT LETTERS

JANNER'S COMPLETE SPEECHMAKER

JANNER'S COMPLETE LETTERWRITER

JANNER ON PRESENTATION

Details about 'Janner's Employment Letters'; Janner's
Cassette Club; and in-company and public courses by
Greville Janner and his colleagues are available from:
Paul Secher, LlB, J.S. Associates, 25 Victoria Street,
London SW1. Telephone (24 hours): 01-222 2102

JANNER
ON
MEETINGS

FOR MY FAVOURITE CHAIRMAN
COUNCILLOR RAY FLINT, JP
AND FOR BETTY
WITH APPRECIATION AND AFFECTION

Janner
on
Meetings

Greville Janner, QC, MP

WILDWOOD
HOUSE

First published in hardback 1986 by
Gower Publishing Company Limited

This paperback edition published 1987 by
Wildwood House Limited
Gower House,
Croft Road,
Aldershot,
Hampshire GU11 3HR,
England.

British Library Cataloguing in Publication Data

Janner, Greville
  Janner on Meetings.
  1. Meetings
  I. Title
658.4'563 AS6

ISBN 0-7045-0557-6

Typeset in Great Britain by Guildford Graphics Limited,
Petworth, West Sussex.
Printed by Billing & Sons Limited, Worcester.

Contents

Foreword

by The Right Honourable Bernard Weatherill, MP, Speaker of the House of Commons

No meeting should be taken for granted. Speakers must learn to judge, to command and to demand the attention of their audiences and those who are privileged to be in the chair must control with concentration, tact and fairness. *Janner on Meetings* explains with clarity, with wisdom and with wit the art and the science of dealing with meetings, from both floor and chair.

As Speaker of the House of Commons, my life is filled with meetings. Some are turbulent, others turgid; some lively and tense, others relaxed and even dull. But the mood of the House may change in a moment and no wise Member, and certainly no Speaker, should ever treat the House with anything but the most profound respect. To underestimate an audience is a sin which experienced Parliamentarians – not least, the author of this book – would never knowingly commit.

Basically, the same principles that apply to meetings of the House, whether in the Chamber or in Committee, apply to other gatherings – individual or private, company or corporate. I recommend Greville Janner's book to all who must partake in them.

Preface

This book is designed to help you to make your meetings successful. By knowing and following certain techniques, you can win almost every occasion. You ignore them at your peril and at that of the case you present or promote.

A meeting is to an audience as food to a gourmet. It may delight and satisfy, or bore and nauseate. This book is offered as your guide to the enjoyment of gatherings – how to make the best of every occasion, for yourself and for those whom you represent.

The Russian poet and critic, Vladimir Mayakovsky, wrote: 'Oh! for just one more conference – on the eradication of all conferences!' Which presents a tantalising prospect for those of us who are doomed to spend too much of our lives attending them. It is also impossible, because people must meet and confer, to exchange ideas, to create or to destroy policies or simply to enjoy each other's company.

So this book explains how best to address a meeting – the basic rules on self-presentation and thinking and speaking on your feet... how to prepare for, to organise and to conduct a meeting... how to win from the chair or from the audience... how to handle the press or to face the camera...

From over a quarter-century of addressing and enduring

meetings, I have culled those essentials with which meeting-mongers should succeed but without which they are certain to fail. They are presented as the meeting itself should be, with a light and varied touch, and in a form intended for reading as well as for reference.

So whether you are coping with close-up communication or a mass meeting ... with a sales presentation or an after-dinner speech ... with a gathering of friends or opponents, shareholders or delegates, family or friends or foes ... here are your basic rules. Minutes, agendas, visual aids ... notes for speakers and for the Chair ... the art of apology and flattery ... the use of wit and of humour ... All are covered, along with the complete range of rules for addressing meetings, keeping order, taking the chair and dealing with a wide variety of specific meetings, with or without visual aids and accessories.

My warm thanks to John Green, for checking the manuscript of the book, and for his advice and friendship.

Greville Janner

PART I

ADDRESSING MEETINGS

1 Think on your Feet!

If your mind works well when your body is seated, why should it go numb when you rise to your feet to face a meeting? When facing an audience, does your stomach rise along with your body, do your heart thump and your tongue cleave to the roof of your mouth? If so, you need to study the rules on how to think on your feet and then to force yourself to apply them at the slightest provocation.

Once you get used to talking upright, it is actually easier than doing it sitting down. Ask lawyers whether they prefer to address a court on their feet or a tribunal from their chairs and they will almost certainly choose to be upright. On your feet, you dominate; on your rear, you are on everyone's level. So rise; forget that your knees are shaking; and stare your audience straight in the eye.

To avoid that eye being glazed, hostile, mocking or all three, choose it with care. 'Even in the most unfriendly audience,' a colleague MP told me, 'you can always find some old dear who'll smile at you! If you can't, then plant one!'

If you look your audience in the eye, your own nervousness will at first go unseen and then disappear.

At the start of your presentation, take command – of yourself and of your audience. Adjust your tie or your dress before you stand and your microphone when you reach it. Take your time before you begin. Wait for silence and full attention – then away you go. As soon as you hear your own voice, firm and friendly, you will start relaxing.

Even if you are making a formal speech in which any false word may be slung back into your teeth, try to avoid word-for-word preparation, like an oratorical plague. Find your words on paper and you will lose your audience. Instead, use notes.

Notes should be brief, clearly legible and written or typed on cards which you can comfortably hold in one hand. Start with your opening, so that your mind will be (literally) reminded of your first words, even if these are only: 'Ladies and gentlemen'.

If you run into protocol, take a leaf out of the toast-master's book and (if necessary with his help) list your listeners: 'Mr President, My Lord Mayor, My Lords, ladies and gentlemen . . .'

Next: Structure your speech. Work out its main points and put each onto a separate card. Create the skeleton of your presentation and flesh it out with words, to fit both the audience and its reaction.

I once asked the redoubtable Lord (Mannie) Shinwell – already well into his nineties – after a brilliant and noteless oratorical performance in Trafalgar Square, whether he ever prepared his speeches, word for word. 'Never,' he replied, 'Not for the last fifty years. I work out half a dozen ideas and then hope for the best. Usually, the words will cascade out when the time comes. Sometimes, of course, they don't . . . You can't win every time, can you?'

I have never seen Shinwell lose on his feet. Those who read their speeches seldom win.

In Parliament, only front benchers at the despatch box are allowed to read their speeches. The rest of us may use notes. If a colleague breaks this rule, someone on the other side is sure to shout out: 'Reading!' – which may sound juvenile when you listen to Question Time on the radio but which really does prevent MPs from being driven out of the chamber by boredom.

In the US Congress, you may submit your speeches

to be inserted into the Record. In our legislature, prepared monotonies designed for repetition in the local press are unappreciated and those who deliver them are commonly called 'Chamber emptiers'!

Once you have prepared and noted the body of your speech, work out its ending. Your first and your last words are the most important. The first create the atmosphere and the last leave your listeners with your message in their minds. Most untrained executives lower their voices at the end of most sentences and leave their audiences on some such unoriginal and crashing anti-climax as: 'Thank you very much for listening to me.' The idea of reaching your climax before your intercourse begins is a curious reversal of nature! Your audience, sir or madam, should be thanking you for addressing them.

The key to confidence is to know both your subject and your audience. The former you can study in advance; the latter will depend not only on persons but on mood. Any professional performer will tell you: 'A story or a joke which brings the house down one night may die on the next.' That is the challenge of performing. As a speechmaker, you perform from your own script.

If you prepare your speech and use your notes as pointers, not crutches, then you are ready to think on your feet. No heckler can throw you off your course, if it is already variable; no interrupter destroy your concentration, if your mind is on your ideas rather than your words.

Speakers always have a vast advantage over those who would destroy them. The audience has come to hear them. The many will not appreciate disturbance by the few. You have (as President Roosevelt put it, in rather different circumstances) nothing to fear but fear itself. Once that is conquered, you win.

Words matter and gestures detract from their impact. So keep still and if you do not know what to do with your hands, press your fingers on the table or on the lectern or put your hands behind your back.

To hold your audience, vary your pace and your material. Watch your listeners and, when their attention wanders, chase them – with an anecdote or an analogy, a joke or a story.

Cast your beady eyes at those who yawn. Do not allow people to talk while you are.

Former 'King Rat', and great entertainer, David Berglas, has a standard routine. 'Can you hear me?' he asks the couple whispering at the back of his audience. 'You can? That's fine. I can hear you too!'

I prefer just to stare at the offenders. If you are free to move, with or without a wandering microphone, stroll in their direction and they will soon stop talking. If your presentation deserves attention, make sure that you get it.

If you cannot be heard, adjust your voice to the acoustics. Move nearer to the microphone or hold it closer to your mouth. Or just imagine that the man at the back of the room is deaf. He may be.

I once studied at Harvard Law School under a brilliant and eccentric lawyer, Judge Manley Hudson, formerly of the International Court of Justice. When he could not hear he would yell out: 'Take your voice and throw it against the wall and make it' – here he paused for both breath and effect and then bellowed out – 'B-O-U-N-C-E off!' Hyperbole, of course – but better that your words should be loudly heard than not at all.

Once you know these rules, practise them on any willing victims you can find. You are invited to your local Rotary Club lunch? Accept. You hear a series of lectures at your local Women's Institute or Church Council? Then offer to give one on your speciality.

Or get yourself trained by experts. Armed with see-yourself-hear-yourself video and recording machinery, my colleagues and I can teach you more in a couple of compressed and comparatively painless days than you could learn in a lifetime of error, causing on each occasion suffering not only to yourself but to your hapless listeners, who are probably undeserving of such treatment.

Too many people in business or in public life are sadomasochists about speeches. Which explains why audiences retreat from lectures and meetings to the safety of the radio and television. At least if a presenter is not switched on, they can forthwith switch him off.

So if you wish to be invited back, prepare and practise

thinking on your feet. As one fuel expert put it: 'If the speaker cannot strike oil, then we shall do our best to see that he stops boring!' Conversely: If you speak well on your feet, others will think well of your case. Speechmaking is an art and the fact that too few are prepared to devote enough time to its study is all to your good if you are prepared to be the exception to this rhetorical rule.

2 Communication

Communication means the transfer of ideas – at its best, in more than one direction. It should have little to do with the customary miserable, monotonous reading of a pre-prepared text to a captive meeting.

Consider, for instance, the prototype deliverer of a vote of thanks. He (or very often nowadays the statutory 'she') produces a closely typed or handwritten document, polished to the last eminently forgettable cliché. The reading begins: 'We thank our distinguished speaker for his brilliant address. It was as we expected – an appeal to all of us to stand up and be counted. In this day and age and at this moment in time, it is up to each and every one of us to respond to our speaker's stirring appeal . . .'

Ernest Bevin referred to that sort of epic as 'clitch after clitch after clitch'! Assuming that the speaker has communicated a message to the audience, there is in the response no hint of any transfer of ideas.

'Well,' you answer, 'that's fine for you as a professional. But it won't do for us executives, forced unwillingly on shaking knees . . .'

Rubbish. With a modicum of training – which most executives are too arrogant or too fearful to acquire – you can at least learn to look as if you were in communication with your audience.

Start with the first sentence. You do not have to be
a rhetorical genius to look up and say: 'Ladies and gentlemen
– That was a marvellous address, wasn't it? We do thank
you, Mr Brown, for your memorable message. We in the
... group/industry/club are fortunate to have induced you
to spend your evening with us.'

Simple, clear words. None of that usual, boring, thought-
less nonsense about 'giving up your valuable time' or 'knowing how busy you are'... Simplicity and sincerity are
apparent synonyms.

Next: As discussed in the last chapter: Look your
audience in the eye. If you peer down and communicate
with your notes on the floor it is as ineffective as to look
up at a screen or a slide or at the ceiling. Tevye the Milkman,
in the immortal *Fiddler on the Roof*, sometimes glanced
upwards to communicate with the Almighty, but he never
lost touch with his earthly audience.

My advice to the communicator-on-the-spot: Imagine
that you are talking one to one, across a coffee table. If
you wish to charm and to convince, look your companion
straight in the eye, chat... be yourself... and recognise that
the eye is the keyhole to the mind. To look away from your
audience is discourteous and (in every sense) uncommuni-
cative.

Then: Be direct. Use the active and not the passive voice
– 'We decided' and not 'It was decided by us'. Say: 'You',
'I' or 'we' and not: 'One'.

There are, of course, limits to these doctrines. You need
not always tell your audience precisely what you think of
them. A gentlemen (or a lady, for that matter) never intention-
ally offends.

An executive said to his assistant: 'You are the biggest
idiot that I have ever met.' His colleague retorted: 'Well,
I have always thought that *you* were one of the best people
to work for. But perhaps we were both wrong!'

Better than calling your audience stupid, try: 'I'm sure
it's my fault. I have clearly not explained myself properly...'
You are probably right.

Communication does not mean constant speech. As John
Le Carré remarked: 'Those with theatrical experience will

know that there is nothing like silence to establish communication.' Nor is there anything like a confident pause to retain it.

A toastmaster once introduced me as follows: 'Ladies and gentlemen, pray for the silence of Mr Greville Janner!' Let no one have to pray for yours – either during your speech or long after it should have come to its intelligent end.

So listen and learn. As Bing Crosby said: 'I listen a lot and talk less. You can't learn anything when you're talking.' We have, after all, two ears and only one mouth, so that we may listen twice as much as we speak.

Columnist Katherine Whitehorn described a good listener as 'not someone who has nothing to say... but a good talker with a sore throat!' The fact that your mind is active does not require you to maintain perpetual speech. To quote again – this time from the Book of Proverbs: 'A fool uttereth all his mind.' A wise man communicates with his ears, teamed with his tongue.

It is accepted wisdom but actual nonsense that communication between management and trade unions in British industry and commerce is generally bad. On the contrary: It is usually good, with convenors and often shop stewards having direct and immediate access to power at the top.

Our exectives' failure is that so often they do not communicate with each other and especially with managers at lower levels. Result: If their colleagues want to know what is going on in the business, they consult trade union leaders, who, if they do not know, can usually and smartly find out.

So when you get an audience at your mercy, do not talk to yourself. If you have problems in thinking on your feet, then take instruction. You may learn through trial and error. The error will then be yours and the trials will be your listeners'!

3 Keys to Conviction

How can you convince a meeting that your view is correct?

Sincerity is the first essential. Laurence Olivier was asked the secret of success on the stage. 'Sincerity, sincerity,' he replied. 'Once you can fake that you can achieve anything!'

If you at least appear to believe in your case, then there is a reasonable chance that your conviction will be shared by your audience. If you do not, you will lose.

If you lean heavily to one viewpoint, say so. 'I will now give you the benefit of my well considered bias' is an excellent line.

Or: 'As our company depends entirely upon this product for its future, I can scarcely be impartial when looking at alternatives . . .'

In the chair, speak straight. 'The decision is one for the Board, and I shall make sure that both sides are well heard. But permit me to express my own view . . .'

Understatement is a far better vehicle for sincerity than exaggeration. Hyperbole kills cases. Accuse a speaker of 'gush', 'melodrama' or 'crocodile tears' and you are scarcely casting compliments.

Listen to any skilled advocate presenting a case to Judge or to jury. It is irrelevant whether the counsel or solicitor believed in that case before the hearing or whether that belief will survive its end. While the battle is on, the advocate must believe in the client's cause, or insincerity will destroy it.

Opponents of a newly-formed political party, whose leadership was made up largely of refugees from their own, quipped that the greatest asset of their former colleagues was that they had 'no previous convictions'! Which makes an excellent beginning for a plea in mitigation, but not for a political party or for a speech. Others will only be convinced of your case if you are. Sincerity is the only truly vital credential.

Lawyers are often asked: 'Would you defend clients whom you know to be guilty?' The best answer is a series of other questions: 'How would I know, unless they tell me – in which case they must either plead guilty or get some other advocate? A client's story is unlikely? Does that make it untrue? Have you never said: 'What an amazing coincidence – no one would ever believe it'? Well, is it for counsel and solicitors to decide on the guilt of their clients – or for the court?'

The answer, of course, is that it is the job of the advocate to put the client's case, at its best and without deceiving the court, but with full force. Where necessary, the skilled lawyer must suspend disbelief while doing the job.

As with the lawyer, so with any other advocate of any cause. You must believe in your case or you will lose it.

Before making a 'plea in mitigation' on behalf of a convicted client, I asked him what he would like me to say for him. 'Just be careful,' he replied. 'If you get a short sentence wrong, I shall get a longer one...' Which reminds me of the Judge who asked a convicted crook: 'Have you anything to say before I pass sentence?' 'Yes, yer Honour,' the man replied. 'For gawd's sake, keep it short!'

Brevity and sincerity are partners in conviction.

Second: Smile. Singapore Airlines are reputed to run a special course to instruct their air hostesses in the art of the eternal smile. The traveller is rude? Smile. She shouts? Smile more. He insults you? Smile again, with understanding. The customer must be tired or unhappy to react so disagreeably.

Alexander Pope wrote: 'Eternal smiles his emptiness betray, as shallow streams run dimpling all the way.' You need what J.M. Barrie described in *Dear Brutus* as 'the same kind, beaming smile that children could warm their hands at.'

Be careful, though, to smile *with* and not *at*. Do not humiliate those whom you need to please.

Your audience must like you. If they trust you personally, then they will accept your message or at least reject it without rancour.

I once asked John Goss, eminent former BBC executive and tutor, how to cope with confrontations. He said: 'Remember that television is a family medium. Imagine the average family group, sitting somewhere behind the cameras. When you are interviewed, you come into their home. They will not expect you, as their guest, to be bullied. Your object is to get them to say: "Well, I may not agree with him, but he has a point . . . and he put it fairly . . ." '

Fairness is best expressed in quiet understatement, not flamboyant hyperbole . . . by speech that is soft and sensible, rather than vituperative or melodramatic. Even genuine tears may look false from a platform or meeting and no medium unmasks the insincere with a surer touch than television.

John Goss again: 'The reason so many TV amateurs appear dishonest is because they do not look the viewer in the eye – especially if they are in some far off studio and speaking "down the line". Remedy: Ask for an "eyeline". The director or producer will tell you where to fix your eyes, so that you appear to be looking straight at the viewer.'

As on TV, so from the platform or table, at a distance or close up, with a large or small or any audience – rapport means (yet again) eye contact. Start by making friends with your audience, then retain their friendship by fixing them, like the Ancient Mariner, with your honest eye.

Now, imprint your message. In the words of that sensible adage: 'Say what you are going to say; then say it; then say what you have said.' Listen to any skilled speaker and wait for the repetition of words, of phrases, of ideas.

The composer of a musical work (other than some of the most modern) will spell out a theme; repeat it, woven with variation and colour, with change of mood and of rhythm; and will then return triumphantly to that theme. So the skilled speaker should spell out the message; explain and expand upon it. Leave the message clearly etched into the minds of the audience, by the final summary, coda and climax.

You must, of course, serve up your meal with an eye to the appetite and to the tastes of your customers. You would scarcely put your message in the same words or tone if (for instance) you were addressing a meeting of managers, staff or workforce as you would if you were conveying even the identical information or message to (say) shareholders or creditors. Horses for courses, dishes for palates, and words for occasions and for audiences.

Be careful, too, how you react to words which you do not fully understand. I remember with vivid misery the occasion in 1946 when I was watching a football match in the Bergen-Belsen displaced persons' camp. My neighbour started chatting to me with animation, but in a language I did not understand. I smiled, helpfully – at which the man became distressed. A friend interpreted: 'He's telling you about the liquidation of his family and he wonders why you are smiling!' I apologised profoundly, and tried not to forget the lesson.

On the platform at a memorial meeting, my neighbour whispered a whimsical story about the deceased. I chuckled. 'What a wit,' I said. I was later criticised for what the army calls 'conduct unbecoming'.

Still: These are the exceptions. The rule for the ruler of a meeting is generally: Keep cool, calm and in smiling good humour yourself and you have a reasonable prospect of extracting the same from others.

Which leads to another key quality: Consideration – for the participants themselves and for the views they express.

An ancient Jewish sage was once threatened with death if he could not sum up the law of God while standing on one leg. 'Do unto others that which thou wouldst have them do unto you', he explained. 'That is the whole of the law. All the rest is commentary.'

Give the same consideration and attention to the opinions of others as you would have them to give to yours.

Most good speakers and all skilled chairmen are excellent listeners.

How, then, do you show your attention to others at speech?

● Look at the speaker and do not yourself talk while you are being talked to.

● Take a careful and obvious note of the speaker's main points. Record making is the sincerest form of flattery.

● If you are actually writing a letter or a shopping list, totting up your debts or (worse) drawing a witty caricature of the speaker, keep the paper well covered. Even if it is invisible to the victim, its contents may be passed on later by a malicious viewer. 'You should have seen what Joe was drawing during your report!'

Finally and above all: in language as in life, truth is beauty, beauty is truth. Your own good name and integrity should convey your conviction. You should study style and technique so that you do not appear unconvincing and emerge with your audience unconvinced. Your case must be sound and it must itself both sound and resound with conviction.

4 The Magic Pause

Timing is the key to successful speaking, and the pause is the secret of good timing. From the start of a speech or presentation until its end, the mastery of the pause is the least practised and most essential element of spoken magic.

That great pianist, Artur Schnabel, once said: 'The notes I handle no better than many pianists. But the pauses between the notes – ah, that is where the art resides!' As with the music of the piano, so with that of the voice. Any amateur idiot can reel off a string of words. It takes a professional with trained self-control to pause between them.

In the beginning, says the Bible, God created the heaven and the earth. Then He added daily to His handiwork, pausing to note the good effect, and that it was morning and it was evening...

The oratorical ungodly rush to their feet... start speaking before they have even stretched their bodies... grab the microphone, which pops back at them, screaming with wrath – and adjust it whilst talking... They look down at their script or notes, and race into disaster, literally without pausing for breath. They do not look at their audience before leaping into the mire.

'It's all nerves!' you say. Agreed. The test of excellence is recognising that nervous tension is the precursor of success.

It releases the adrenalin which sharpens the mind. Top performers – artistes, athletes or orators – worry if they are
not nervous.

Once you recognise and welcome the inevitable, you
can deal with it. As already suggested :get to your feet slowly;
adjust your microphone; survey your audience, eye to eye;
wait for silence and for attention. Then, and only then, begin.

'Ladies . . .' pause 'and . . .' pause 'Gentlemen . . .'. Not
– 'Ladiesandgentlemen . . .'

So, once more: never start speaking until you have command of both your audience and yourself. Once you hear
your own voice emerging, measured and with authority, you
will lose all fear.

Listen to the stage compère, the ringmaster, the professional presenter . . . the toastmaster . . . 'My Lords . . .
ladies . . . and gentlemen . . . Pray silence for . . . our guest
of honour . . . Mrs . . . Hermione . . . White . . .' Each word
counts and the pause leads into it.

The same principle applies both to TV and to radio
interviews. Not long ago, I was given my own 'spot' on
a political TV programme. For once the roles were to be
reversed, the biter bit, the interviewee to do the interviewing
with a professional by his side.

When I had finished interviewing police and public,
I asked my minder: 'How was it?'

'Fine,' he said. 'But when you do it again, give them
breathing time.'

I had been so concerned with silence that, when I
thought that my victim had dried up, I had repeated the
question or asked another one. I had forgotten to give the
questioned the right to breathe. I had forgotten the weight
of silence, the value of the interval, the need to take breath.

In courts, and in tribunals, do not be afraid to wait
and to think.

Speakers should not talk while they look down at their
notes. Give the audience time to shift around in its seat
and it will be grateful. Pour on with your torrent of words
and you will drown the listening minds.

The end of the speech should convey your message and
give your audience future cause and pause for thought. Forget

that awful 'thank-you-very-much-ladies-and-gentlemen-for-listening-to-me'. If you have done your job properly, they will be thanking you, not you them. Instead, rise to your crescendo. Then stop.

There are, of course, limits to the successful pause, as there are to all other techniques. Not long ago, a parliamentary colleague was chided by Mr Speaker Weatherill for going on too long. 'But Mr Speaker,' he protested, 'I have only spoken for a short time.' 'It is the pauses in your speech that have taken too long!' Mr Speaker retorted.

Speaker Weatherill was right. The MP had fumbled with notes and with words alike, leaving his audience irritated and bored. Most had only stayed in the Chamber because they were themselves hoping to catch the Speaker's eye. MPs of all parties object to length of wind, especially when they hold their own in check.

5 Time – the Enemy

Time management is a skill which some of us enjoy by instinct; which others have the humility to learn; but which few apply to their speeches or presentations. From Parliament to parish pump, from great oration to brisk harangue, time is the enemy unrecognised.

Most speeches and presentations take longer to make than their rehearsal suggests. Allow for interruptions – questions, perhaps, or if you are lucky, applause... and for your ideas to develop, as you think on your feet.

Adjust length to audience. Even a small turnout is entitled to a decent delivery. But why not shorten the formalities and stretch the time for discussion or questions?

A vicar in a country parish noticed that only one farmer had turned up for evensong. He trudged regardless through the entire service, including a twenty-minute sermon, as if the place were packed.

As the lone parishioner left, the vicar smiled at him and said: 'I do hope that you enjoyed the service?' 'When there is only one cow in the field,' the farmer intoned, 'you still have to feed him, don't you? But you don't have to give him the full load of hay, do you?'

If your audience becomes restless, either wind up or change tack or momentum. Introduce humour... tell a story ... or use that most masterful trick of the confident speaker – involve your audience. 'What do you think of that proposition? How many of you have experienced this problem?'

Numbers are irrelevant. Copy the skilled cabaret artist. Extract response from one of your audience and the rest will be riveted.

When reacting to your audience, watch out for *its* attention to time. A professor noticed a student checking his watch. 'Now then, Mr Jones,' he said, 'I don't mind you looking at your watch. But when you hold it up to your ear and shake it, then I get worried ...!'

Do not make your speeches too long because you fear that you may end too early. Ask yourself: How often have you complained that someone else's speech ended too soon?

If you are in the chair, then to avert time troubles:

● Recognise that most speakers overrun. Always ask for a shorter time than you want. Any balance can be used for questions or discussion ...

● Say to the speaker *in advance*: 'You kindly agreed to talk for twenty minutes. Would you like me to give an indication when you have two or three minutes to go?' Most gladly agree. The rest are a pain and should not be re-invited.

● Pass a clearly visible note to the speaker whose time is up. 'THREE MINUTES – PLEASE' or 'SORRY – PLEASE END'. Unless you wish to be disliked, do so inconspicuously, and preferably at a pause for breath or for consulting notes.

Prepare for your own time problems by using one or all of the following methods:

● Prop up your watch, clearly visible in front of you. If it boasts an alarm, you could set it to (say) five minutes after you should have wound up.

● Ask the chairman for an indication as your time limit approaches.

● Ask your wife or husband or colleague or an employee to mark time for you – visibly and clearly . . .

● Do not denounce the chairman who draws your attention to overrunning. Do not say: 'I have come all the way from Paris to speak to you and the chairman is trying to stop me . . .' Or: 'I have been told I must finish. So I must leave out the crucial part of my message . . .' Or even worse: 'The chairman has asked me to stop; I ask you to let me go on . . .' The chairman squirms and exodus begins.

● Do not speed your delivery, to pack more words into the same time. You will fail. Instead, summarise your points; pretend that you have structured your address so as to fit into the time provided – and leave extra time for your peroration and for the applause which you have earned through your consideration for the time of your audience. With that lack of balanced judgement common to most audiences, they will regard their time as of equal value to your own.

● In the long run: Train yourself to recognise and to sense the passing of time.

Playwright Eugene Ionesco said, 'We haven't the time to take our time.' Nor do we have the right to requisition other people's.

Adlai Stevenson once apologised for arriving late at a campaign rally. 'The worst thief,' he proclaimed, 'is the one who takes someone else's time. That, after all, is the one commodity that can never be recovered.'

Treasure the time of others as you would your own. Speak unto them as thou wouldst that they should speak unto thee – briefly.

Sir Osbert Sitwell wrote of Mrs Southern:

She did not recognise her enemy,
She thought him Dust:
But what is Dust,
Save Time's most lethal weapon,
Her faithful ally and our sneaking foe?

Those who address meetings or make presentations and who do spare the time to make it a 'faithful ally' should succeed. Those who fail to recognise it as a foe, sneaking and dangerous, invite failure – for themselves, for the case they present and for the company they keep or represent.

6 Wit and Humour

Wit and humour brighten any meeting. There is an art to both.

Wit is the spice of good speech. Use it with skill and discretion and it will banish dullness, puncture stress and breathe life into the most miserable occasion. You abuse it at your own risk.

The best humour is immediate, reactive and topical. It emerges from the moment with apparent spontaneity. The sharp response to an interruption or the unexpected reference to the name of the venue or even to the event of the day may seem weak in retrospect, but will bring a chuckle or even a cheer at the time.

Refer to the speech that preceded yours. Use your introduction to spark off your opening. With experience, you learn to keep some standard response at the ready.

For instance: I am still frequently introduced as the son of my late and distinguished father. I then thank my introducer on behalf of my father and myself, and enquire gently which of us they thought would be addressing them. Then I mention a letter that I once received and which remains framed in my home. The correspondent took no chances. It is addressed to: 'The Right Hon. Lord Greville Janner, QC, MP'. It begins: 'Dear Sir or Madam'!

The best humour is topical. The worst is offensive. Poke

fun at yourself, but leave jokes about others to them. Poor
taste is seldom forgiven.

In general, leave Irish jokes to the Irish; but no one
objects to the friendly and the whimsical. For instance, if
you are either starting late or determined to be brief, tell
them about the man who aked the Irish Professor: 'What
is the Gaelic for "mañana"?' The Professor replied: 'In the
Irish language, we have no word which expresses quite that
sense of urgency!'

Or if you are drawing attention to the goodwill of the
occasion, use Samuel Johnson's marvellous description of
the Irish: 'They are a fair minded people. They seldom speak
well of each other!'

Mind how you speak ill of your audience, even in jest.
When I lecture on law or on presentation, I invariably tease
my audience. I apologise in advance. I tell them how I once
ironically asked a man who had given a particularly cunning
answer to a question: 'And when, sir, were you last in prison?'
'I was released three weeks ago!' he replied. You tread on
the dignity of others at your risk.

To use humour effectively, you must combine two con-
flicting elements: familiarity and recognition on the one hand
and surprise on the other.

An audience needs to know when it is expected to laugh.
A satirical radio programme recently put out a spoof edition
which included an alleged interview with one of my assistants.
'How does this man manage to be in five places at once?'
asked the interviewer. 'Well, he uses a cardboard cut-out.
Or sometimes his son, Daniel, will go in his place. It's all
really an illusion. He's a member of the Magic Circle,' came
the reply.

The interview continued in light, satirical vein – which
would have been fine, had the audience known that it was
the equivalent of an April Fool's Day send-up.

While the humorous speakers must not collapse in
laughter at their own jokes, they should usually smile or
otherwise indicate to their audience that they are jesting.
But equally, it is the element of surprise that brings down
the house, particularly when the joke has an extra sting in
a second tail.

Take, for instance, the story told to me by a Conservative Cabinet Minister of the alleged occasion when Prime Minister Thatcher met President Mitterrand and President Reagan. 'I've got a problem,' said Reagan. 'I've twenty-three body-guards and one of them is KGB. And I cannot find out which one it is.'

'My problem is worse,' said the French President. 'I have twenty-three mistresses. One of them is not faithful to me. And I cannot find out which one it is.'

'I envy you your problems,' said the Prime Minister. 'I have twenty-three people in my Cabinet. One of them is quite clever. And I cannot find out which one it is . . .!'

Or try the favourite story of former Lord Chancellor, the genial Elwyn Jones. He tells of the occasion when a Judge was swearing in a jury somewhere in the West Country. A prospective juryman said: 'My lord, please may I be excused from jury duty?'

'What is your reason, Mr Jones?' asked the Judge.

'My wife,' said the man, 'is about to conceive!'

Then Elwyn pauses for laughter before adding the ulti-mate punch line.

'Mr Jones,' said the Judge. 'I do not think that is what you really mean. I think that what you mean is that your wife is about to be confined. But Mr Jones . . . whether you are right or I am right . . . I do agree that you should be there!'

Timing and confidence are the twin keys to success with humour – plus experience. Do not be afraid of the after-dinner speech. Practise it. If giving a serious talk, anywhere other than at a funeral, slot in some humour. The less it is expected and the more boring the occasion, the more it will be appreciated.

Finally: If humour fails, switch off. Do not be upset. Audiences vary with fickle and unpredictable mood.

So if your audience is in no mood for humour, go serious. If it begins to yawn, brighten its mood with a joke or a jibe, a tale or a twist. Watch your audience like a hawk or your humour will drop like a stone from the sky.

7 Laugh – at your own Expense

Make fun at yourself at a meeting and no one else will be offended.

The art of self-deprecation is splendidly British. Knowing as we do that both Britain and the British are best, we can make as much fun as we like of ourselves, without the least anxiety. The fact that others may take us seriously is because they have the misfortune to be foreigners.

Addressing a French audience in Strasbourg, seat of the European Parliament, I was asked by the charming wife of President Pierre Pflimlin: 'M. Janner, what is your origin?'

I replied: 'Je m'excuse ... pardonnez-moi ... I am British ... But it is not my fault!' The place exploded with delight.

I continued: 'However, I was born in Cardiff ... I am Welsh ... and the Welsh are the cream of British Society ... In our own mind, if not that of anyone else ... We are, if you like, the Strasbourgeois of the United Kingdom.'

The converse of running yourself down is, of course, playing your audience up. No one spurns flattery. Israeli Parliamentarian Abba Eban, who is one of the world's most accomplished speakers, once responded to a particularly flowery introduction thus: 'I thank you very much for those wonderful compliments. No politician can afford to be other than grateful for compliments, however undeserved. We receive them too rarely!'

Self-deprecation is easy for politicians because everyone so readily deprecates us. Thus: 'I suppose you know the definition of a statesman? A dead politician.' Cheers and counter-cheers ... Or: 'A politician is, of course, a person who speaks while others sleep ...'

I took some American guests around Westminster Abbey. I showed them the inscription on the tomb of a deceased colleague: 'Here lies a great politician and an honest man,' it read. A guest exclaimed: 'I did not know that in Britain you buried two people in the same grave!'

As I am also a lawyer, I have no shortage whatever of self-deprecatory material. My favourite is the story of the man who went to his local Law Society and asked to be recommended to a one-armed lawyer. 'Why do you want a one-armed lawyer?' 'Because,' he replied, 'I am sick to death of being told: "On the one hand this, on the other hand that!"'

Still: I advise you not to tell jokes like that to an audience of lawyers. We may be offended because we have a very high opinion of ourselves. Someone has to.

In reality, we lawyers are extremely witty. Nor do we lose our sense of humour when we acquire security, distinction and a satisfactory pension by accepting an appointment as a Judge. While it is a basic rule of advocacy not to make jokes of your own, but to laugh heartily at those of the person who will decide upon the fate of your client and your case, Judges feel free to make fun of anyone they wish. Provided that you are not that person, judicial wit may add much-needed spice to an otherwise dreary proceeding.

Defamation actions are an orator's dismay. Many an elegant phrase or slip of the wit has landed the joker in court. The action for libel or slander is the citizen's defence against misplaced jokes, oral or (worse) written. And while 'mere vulgar abuse' is (believe it or not) a good defence 'I thought it was funny, didn't you?' is not.

Like Parliamentarian Jonathan Aitken, who was sued for comparing a constituent and fellow Conservative to a florid and somewhat drunken character in a current soap opera. She sued and lost, but not before he had suffered the usual miseries and costs of litigation.

Afterwards, a journalist inquired what he thought of the plaintiff. He quoted Groucho Marx: 'If I never see her again, it will be too soon!'

The speaker, like the writer, should guard his lips from guile and his tongue from ill judged jokes. Unless they are at his own expense, they may be just that!

8 'Upstaging'

Alas for Indira Gandhi! She was not only a redoubtable lady on stage. Off stage, she was a gracious and kindly hostess and a warm and generous person. She once proved herself world champion in that essential art of upstaging, so vital at any meeting.

It was 1978 and Mrs Gandhi was in prison. Her rival and former colleague, Charan Singh, held a massive outdoor rally.

From her cell, Mrs Gandhi arranged for a huge bunch of red roses to be taken up onto the platform and presented to Charan Singh, with her love. The audience was riveted; the media were entranced. Mrs Gandhi and her roses stole Charan Singh's show, TV and all.

Variants of the same technique can and should be applied by executives and public figures, absent or in person. They require flair and forethought.

My colleague, Joe Ashton, MP, served his apprenticeship in politics with a brilliant old Jewish councillor called Issy Lewis, who taught him the art of 'tummling'. Like a political magician, Lewis diverted the eyes of the public from centre stage while he got his own way unobserved. Example: Lewis wished to impose a mighty increase in local rates. He included an extra charge of a modest penny for the use of public

lavatories. The row then centred on the indescribable wicked-
ness of the new bowel tax. When in due course the councillor
bowed with democratic dignity to public outrage and withdrew his shameful proposal, everyone had forgotten about
the main and far more unpleasant increase in overall taxation.

The old councillor was on stage, front and centre. But
what of the executive art of being in two places at once
– or, as Issy Lewis might have put it, the problem of dancing
at two simultaneous weddings with the same pair of feet?
I recommend the marvel performed by the Biblical Enoch.
All other characters in that book duly died. But not Enoch.
'And he was no more', we are told. He simply disappeared,
without trace or warning.

Forced to leave an important meeting early and not want-
ing my absence to be noted, I checked that the speaker's
rostrum was on the right of the platform and I arranged
to sit on a chair on the far left. When my own speech ended,
I resumed my place. When the next speaker approached the
microphone and all eyes were to the right, I vanished to
the left, mysteriously and unnoticed, taking my chair with
me. I was no more!

Upstaging may also require the substitution of characters, as distinguished visitors to Moscow learned when they
were invited to a local circus. 'Here in the Soviet Union',
said the host, 'we have taught the lion to lie down with
the lamb.' There, in a huge cage and surrounded by an admir-
ing throng, they saw a lion stretched out in one corner and
a lamb in the other.

'Amazing!' proclaimed the visitors. 'How do you do it?'

'No problem,' replied the host. 'We replace the dead
lamb every morning!'

Of course, dead lambs tell no tales and can scarcely
express their indignation. Upstaged human beings are different. Still, if the job is done with dignity they may, however
grudgingly, salute professionalism and learn their lesson. As
another medical sage put it: 'If you are proved right, you
accomplish little; but if you are proved wrong, you gain much
– you learn the truth!'

The best upstaging is by birth. When the late Aga Khan
was to be guest at a luncheon in the House of Lords, the

host wrote for guidance at to precedence to the repository of all such knowledge, the Garter King of Arms. After a long wait, he received the following reply: 'The Aga Khan is believed to be a direct descendant of God. English dukes take precedence . . .!'

You may attempt a similar process by speaking in a language which you presume that your listeners will not understand. A Canadian executive once commented on this technique, in response to a suggestion that the proceedings of the meeting ought to be held from time to time in French. He said: 'If the English language was good enough for Matthew, Mark, Luke and John, it will do for us.'

The best upstaging evokes admiration, not offence. But if you do cause hurt, then apologise – and sidle out of the limelight. If you have won your argument and destroyed your opposition, move on.

Better, though, to choose your methods with care and sensitivity. For instance, had Mrs Gandhi presented Charan Singh with anything other than roses, the gesture might have been undignified, unworthy and either unpublished or harmful. A telegram or a message may bring more limelight to absentees than their presence – especially if they would not have the chance to speak.

I received my final and saddest letter from Mrs Gandhi, written and posted a few days before her murder. It arrived in her usual air mail envelope, complete with seal, stamped: 'Prime Minister's House'. Like love and legends, the great live on – centre stage in history.

9 Ruffled Feathers

Recognising that there is no hell like a colleague scorned and that the unwilling ruffling of feathers is the lot of each of us, consider how to smooth them.

First object: To recognise both the disease of the humbled human and its carrier. Whom have you offended and how?

Some victims may inform you, directly or indirectly. Always be observant and if in doubt send out a scout. 'I noticed that John was unusually silent . . . Mary was glaring at me from the back . . . Can you find out what's wrong?'

Once the disease is identified, attack it with despatch. Alternatives:

- 'I'm told that I offended you by . . . I'm very sorry . . .'

- Pass the apology through an ally. 'I suppose you do know that when Jack said . . . he was not referring to you, but to Bill . . .'

- Make immediate amends. 'I was not able to call Roger to speak earlier. I will do so now . . . with my apologies to him . . .'

The more truly distinguished the dignitaries and the greater their real security, the more likely they are to be generous with your errors. Michael Sacher, a director of Marks and Spencer, arrived at a dinner that I once disorganised, to find that his name had been omitted from the seating plan. Instead of walking out, as I have seen other, lesser, people do in precisely those circumstances, he smiled, shrugged and said to me: 'Never mind. I'm sure someone won't turn up and I'll have his seat.' I had an extra chair put at the top table. I have not forgotten his understanding.

Conversely: The less secure individuals will seek offence. Be sure that he or she who seeketh will find.

If you offend your enemies, then your tactics may be different. Someone once told Ernest Bevin that his arch rival, Herbert Morrison, was 'his own worst enemy'. 'Not while I'm alive, he ain't!' Ernie growled.

If your enemy retaliates, or if you yourself are the victim of attack from any other source, the best response is generally also the most dignified. 'I'm sure that Mr Brown did not intend any personal offence, so let me reply to the points he has made...' Or: 'I hope that on reflection Jane will think better of her remarks. Anyway: Let me try to explain the situation once again.'

You could even try a most effective gambit, taking the blame, especially if everyone, even including the victim, knows that you are blameless, thus: 'I'm so sorry that I did not explain the point clearly... My fault, I'm sure...' Or: 'I know that if I had put the point clearly, Mr Brown would not have taken offence. I'm sorry. Let me try again...' Or even: 'I'm so sorry that Jane took offence when none was intended. If it was my fault, I apologise...'

Then make amends. Try the handsome compliment, deserved or otherwise: 'Mr Brown is a mighty worker for the cause and I would certainly not wish to have offended him.' Or: 'Let me take this opportunity to congratulate Jane on her work in connection with... She has done a marvellous job.'

If you are in the chair, you may make further amends by calling on the victim to speak or maybe to propose the vote of thanks.

If all your efforts to soothe the disgruntled fail, join the club. You will then continue to be criticised and can content yourself with the thought that the only way you may sometimes avoid criticism is to do nothing – but for that you will also be criticised, and with good reason.

Which leaves only one other alternative: To laugh off the entire occasion, turing the joke onto yourself and hoping that the victim will be prepared to forgive the discomfort. 'I hope you have forgiven me for the time when...' is a good line.

Finally: What of the person who may be offended when he finds out about an unintended *faux pas*, committed in his or her absence? There is one answer only: On the first possible occasion, whether in person or by telephone, explain.

I once arranged for an eminent businessman and philanthropist to be invited to an important dinner as my personal guest. His name duly appeared on both list and table plan.

On the evening, a total stranger appeared, a well dressed and personable young man with a Canadian accent. I greeted him with apparent warmth. 'Forgive me, but I don't know your name,' I said. He introduced himself by the same name as the person whom I had intended to invite! He had a lovely evening – and I immediately telephoned my would-be guest, who has ever since enjoyed teasing me about the error. 'I'm still hungry,' he says.

Good humour is the best answer to ill treatment.

In the end, though, there is no better way to calm the waters than by pouring on the oil before they get too rough. Where you can anticipate an attack, puncture the balloon before it rises.

For instance: I was once President of an organisation which ran a wonderfully ambitious reception at Hampton Court Palace, with Prince Charles and Princess Diana as our guests. Everything that could go wrong duly did.

On a June day, it was cold and rainy outside, but stifling hot within. The traffic seized up, so the royal couple arrived over half an hour late. At the reception for members of the organisation and their spouses, there was only one serving table for hundreds of hungry mouths. Many reached it only to find that the food had almost run out – only cold salmon, boiled potatoes and lettuce were left and the strawberries were bereft of cream.

When eventually I led their Royal Highnessess through a corridor gauntlet of adoring subjects, they spoke to many. Others were invisible in both directions.

As for the presentation and speeches, the microphone was missing. I bellowed my words of welcome and the Prince replied with cool and good-humoured aplomb. When I asked him whether he had ever spoken unheard, he replied: 'No – nor unseen!'

Result: As expected, some friends and treasured colleagues rallied around and made the best of the extraordinary evening, laughing off the mishaps and passing their condolences to me in private, but others lashed out – publicly and (in some cases) to the press. Indeed, I heard later that some of the ill will had arisen directly from 'leakages' by a person whom we had employed for the evening and whom I would not willingly take on again.

Question: What to do about the press? Answer: Make the best of it and under no circumstances advertise your errors. As the President and therefore the person responsible, I would accept that responsibility in full, irrespective of fault. To the public, the spilt milk must be made as invisible as possible.

As for the next meeting of the organisation, the tactic was clear:

● First: A complete but dignified apology, identifying myself and my fellow 'top brass' with the feelings of those who had suffered. 'I am so very sorry that colleagues and their guests suffered such inconvenience and disappointment.'

● Second: Responsibility. 'I accept full responsiblity for all that went wrong and my apology is personal.'

● Third: Mitigation – but without placing reservations on the apology – plus a touch of humour. 'It is true that not all the miseries were of our making. The weather ... leading to the delay in the arrival of our guests ... the catering and the caterers ...'

● Fourth: Future action – we decided against an 'enquiry',

which would have kept the wounds open and given scope for the making of hay by those who would have enjoyed it. Instead: 'We are dealing now with the caterers. In our view, there was no excuse either for the inordinate queueing, nor still less, for food running out' (hear, hear – at last, unanimity).

Then the positive: 'I am pleased to tell you that their Royal Highnesses have indicated – both directly and indirectly – that they enjoyed the evening. I am sure that it would be the wish of everyone here that I should convey to them on behalf of us all our very great appreciation not only for being our guests, but for their patience, understanding and marvellous good nature. It was an example to us all.'

In that last half sentence lay the only counter-attack which I regarded as acceptable.

10 Error and Apology

Musician and wit Larry Adler once remarked: 'Vasectomy means not ever having to say you're sorry!' If executives and politicians – especially when speaking or chairing meetings – admitted fault more often, they would be more popular and better trusted. *Mea culpa*, in whatever language, should not be a phrase confined to the prayer meeting.

Suppose that you are selling an idea or a policy, or a proposal or a product. Among the questions you invite at the end, there is almost certain to be at least one that is either plain daft or which shows that the questioner was enjoying sleep more than your talk.

If you are the boss dealing with a subordinate who needs a lesson, or a politician out to down an opponent, then you could try the truth. A respected friend achieved this purpose with a manager by replying to an offensive question thus: 'I know why Joe asked that question. He hopes to become a partner – when he grows up!'

Political savagery, especially in the Chamber of the House of Commons and in Select Committees, is part of the game. Politicians exchange insult without rancour. Opponents frequently respect and like each other, even if they delight in publicly reducing that other's political stature.

The pages of Hansard and corridors of legend resound

to tales of fierce opponents. My favourite was committed
by old Winston Churchill, at his ferocious best. A Labour
MP, unhappily named Will Paling, called Churchill a 'dirty
dog'. The Chamber rang with Tory cries of 'Withdraw, withdraw . . .'

Churchill leaned on the despatch box. 'I do not ask
the honourable Member to withdraw,' he said. 'I . . . er, er . . .
invite him instead . . . to repeat his remark . . . er, er . . . outside
this Chamber . . . and I will then . . . er, er, show him precisely
what . . . er, a dirty dog does to a paling!'

The wise executive will store away this sort of tactic
until elected to Parliament and will then use it only with
care. It would inevitably be a far better response even to
the stupid and ignorant question to take the blame for its
asking.

The more ludicrous the query, the more important it
becomes to save the face of the questioner. This will not
only please him or her but reassure colleagues and fellow
listeners that you are a person of decent compassion and
of compassionate decency.

Thus (and as discussed in the last chapter): 'I am sorry,
but obviously I have not made myself clear. Let me try
again . . .' Or: 'Thank you for that question. I did try to
explain the huge complexities of this subject, but I have
obviously failed. Let me have another go. Please would you
look again at page 12 of our proposal . . .' Or: 'Thank you
for giving me the chance to go over again that crucial part
of my speech. I hope you will excuse my failure to make
everything clear at the first attempt, but . . .'

Honour is satisfied. You can re-emphasise your message.

The more important the questioners, in their own eyes
or in that of their audience, the more vital it becomes to
retain their goodwill by helping to cover up their ignorance
or inattention. Equally, if the point is raised by juniors, whose
future may depend upon seniors within hearing, they will
appreciate your self-restraint as much as they would never
forget or forgive a taunt.

To accept responsibility yourself for a question which
others will see as not very bright will encourage those others
to intervene, with their own comments or queries. Converse-

ly: If you have humiliated a colleague, others will reasonably fear the same treatment. Apprehension will presage silence – a response which is death to any presentation, doom to any meeting.

The more unpopular your case, the more sensible this approach. You want your hearers to say: 'Well, I am not sure that I agree with him, but at least he is not disagreeable.' Or: 'I don't agree with his point of view, but we must take it into account...' Or: 'I think he's wrong, but he's put the point very fairly... and I would be happy to have him as a colleague... adviser... or (even) as my Member of Parliament...'

An organisation called Moral Rearmament achieved vast membership in postwar Britain, largely on a platform of: 'When you are wrong, admit it.' It was itself too often wrong to survive in the political world, but its general premise that it is better deliberately to admit your own failings than to humiliate others by revealing theirs still makes sound sense, at least in this area of presentational skill.

J.B. Priestley once said that he felt apologetic whenever he went into his tailor's shop because he was like a tone deaf hater of classical music spending an evening with a renowned string quartet. At least he made his tailor happy!

P.G. Wodehouse suggested that it is a good rule in life never to apologise. 'The right sort of people', he alleged, 'do not want apologies. The wrong sort take mean advantage of them!'

He was wrong. There is an ancient, proud and diligently sustained parliamentary tradition that those who mislead the House and apologise are forgiven. The rest are not. Unlike politicians, executives are seldom perfect. So a little practice in the art of wise apology would go far towards victories and friendships, deserved or otherwise, and towards convincing meetings that, even if your case is bad, you are not.

'The beauty of making a mistake', Oscar Wilde once remarked, 'is that you can recognise it when you make it again!' If it is someone else's error, then that recognition may be even more rueful. Either way, the happy alternative is to learn from it. Where the error is yours, you should at least know how to pick yourself and (in the context of meetings) your audience and your purpose up from the floor, before you are out for the oratorical count.

Travelling through Asia in the footsteps of Prime Minister Margaret Thatcher, I laughed merrily at the story of her famous *faux pas* when addressing an audience in Indonesia. 'Here in Malaysia', she said. 'Indonesia, dear', husband Denis prompted her from the side. 'Thank you, dear', she said, frostily. Laughter reverberated across the world.

The following day, jet-lagged and dragged from sleep at 6.45 a.m., I broadcast to the nation of New Zealand from a brisk, workmanlike Wellington studio. 'The view from here in Australia,' I said. Ugh! 'And especially in New Zealand,' I continued, hastily. I had recognised the Thatcherite error, in time to squirm my way past it. Had my visit been more publicised, the gaffe would not have passed unremarked.

No such retreat is possible if you talk about 'here in England', when you happen to be in Scotland. In that case, you can only smile and apologise. 'Sorry – I forgot for a moment that I was in the civilised part of the UK.' Apology plus compliment induce forgiveness.

'Sorry. I'll read that again,' says the newscaster who falters. The same approach rarely fails the Chair.

A participant correctly raises a point of order, showing that you have messed up the procedure? Say: 'Sorry – I got that wrong. Let's try again.' Then do it the right way.

If the slip goes unnoticed, you are lucky. Like the actor who fluffs a line, improvises, ad libs . . . carry on and the odds are that your audience will either remain unknowing or forgive, uncaring.

The great Parliamentary tradition, though, is to make a full and frank apology. If an MP misleads the House, he makes a personal statement. This is invariably greeted from all sides with an accepting rumble of 'hear hear'.

The unforgivable is to lie. The hapless John Profumo, the Defence Minister who slid from the paths of righteousness into the bed of a prostitute, did not lose his job for immorality. That offence is frequently forgiven by colleagues grateful that they have not themselves been caught. His crime: that he did not own up . . . did not apologise . . . but, instead, tried to mislead the House, through blatant untruth.

11 Interruptions and Hecklers

For politicians, the only enjoyable elections are those which they either cannot win or cannot lose. The second are the better, if you value your career. It is far more pleasant to be generous in victory than in defeat.

Still there is a magnificent joy in the unwinnable battle. You know that you are about to be destroyed, so you relax and enjoy it in a Confucian manner. Which is how I felt in 1955 when, as a raw youngster, I almost halved the Conservative majority for the suburban seat of Wimbledon, losing by a mere 12,000! My meetings were packed because my friends and I toured the area, calling out on our loudspeakers: 'Come and heckle the Labour candidate! Hecklers welcome!'

Skilled speakers welcome those who feed life into their meetings by attacking them. The person with the platform – especially when clutching the mighty mike – should never lose.

Every interruption at any meeting should be turned to immediate and to good use. Hurl back the taunt at your opponent and, unless the audience has been packed by the enemy, it will rally to your side. Even a hostile meeting will generally give you a fair hearing, if it feels that your are entitled to one.

How, then, do outstanding speakers deal with those who heckle?

● They ask for a courteous hearing. 'Please be good enough to listen to my case. You may find that you agree with it . . .' 'It is only fair that you should listen to my argument, before you decide to disagree . . .'

● They bring the audience onto their side by appealing to their sense of fairness. 'Madam, you are preventing others from hearing the case . . .' 'That's not fair, is it?' – a rhetorical question. Then someone may shout out: 'Of course it is. Your argument is rubbish!' More likely, though, the people around the interrupter will demand: 'Oh, do be quiet . . .' Or: 'Sit down and shut up!'

● They appeal to the Chair to take control. 'I am in your hands, Mr Green. If you and the meeting wish me to continue to explain my case, I will gladly do so. But if it is your wish or the determination of the meeting that I shall not be given a fair hearing, then so be it . . .' You then sit; Mr Green rises from his chair. If the meeting collapses the fault is his and not yours.

The best reaction depends upon the size and the type of the meeting. While brawls may be common at political shindigs, they are not uncommon at some company meetings, particularly where shareholders are dissatisfied with the running of the business. When profits are good and dividends high, meetings are pleasant. When the receiver or liquidator is in the offing or (worse) in the room, sweet nature goes sour . . . The heckler has his or her day and all is darkness for the speaker who cannot handle disaffection.

There are, of course, other interruptions than heckling, far more common and far less difficult to control, if your mind and your tongue are flexible. Never fear to pause. Always make use of the interruption for your own purposes. A pleasant and even witty reference to the moment will be received with appreciation and (often) with laughter, far in excess of its humorous worth. Your audience salutes your oratorical footwork.

An aircraft roars overhead, drowning your words? Stop. 'Could that be . . .' – naming your least favourite airline, perhaps that of the next door nation – 'intent on destroying this gathering, by foul means or fair?'

Or: 'Welcome . . .' naming your favourite airline. 'You have saved my argument from imminent collapse! Thank you . . .'

If your words were not previously well received, you will have a second chance. When the noise has gone, you say: 'All right. So let me tackle the argument from a different angle. Perhaps it will appeal to you more than the last one.'

Someone wheels in a tea trolley, clattering the cups. Pause and thank her. Wait for silence.

A door slams or a passer-by shouts. Beam in if you can and turn the interruption to your credit and to that of your argument.

Experience will teach you when to ignore the interruption. This may be the best tactic if:

- The interruption is minor and the moment significant; even the smallest discordant note may destroy your peroration and blunt the impact of your message. On balance, you may prefer to proceed.

- The meeting is already on your side . . . your argument goes well . . . and the interruption will simply break the flow. In this case try to reach a natural pause before you break the thread of your yarn.

- The interruption is deliberate and its impact can either be postponed or turned to your own purposes. Then say (generally) to the interrupter: 'I am coming to that point. Please be patient . . .' Or, in Parliamentary style: 'I will gladly give way when I have completed this part of my argument.' By that time, your interrupter may have decided to leave you alone or you may have another chance to refuse to accept the break in your argument. Either way, you have won. And winning in this respect as in all others, either is or should be the object of all who spend their time at meetings.

12 The Speaker's Checklist

Are you speaking at a meeting? Then here is your checklist. Go through it with care before you reach the meeting and you will multiply your chances of emerging in good array.

- Have you prepared your subject? Do you know your case? Have you decided how best to present it?

- Have you identified your allies – and primed them to assist, whether by adding their voices or their applause or by asking the questions which will help? And what of your opponents or enemies – how will you best deal with and disarm them?

- Have you prepared yourself? Are you equipped with the necessary notes, documentation, visual aids? What will you wear to suit the occasion, the audience, the image you will wish to project?

- Who will introduce you and how? Should you provide a c.v. or a note, or details of points that you would like the chair or the introducer to make, so as to bolster your case or to help you to make your point?

- What time should you arrive? Should you check the venue, the microphone or other equipment, the seating arrangements? If not, then who will do it for you and whom do you bring with you to act as your assistant, organiser, aide, ears or liaison?

● Have you consulted your colleagues and allies – and the meetings' organisers, if they are on your side – to work out how best to put across your message?

PART II

RULES
AND ORDER

13 On the Agenda

An agenda is to a meeting as a map to a mountaineer. Essential.

You would not think of starting a business day without a planning diary. So why face a meeting without its equivalent?

My late father, Lord (Barnett) Janner packed his diary with intricate scrawl. Watching him at a meeting, a colleague said: 'What are you doing, Barney? Looking to see where you're going next?' 'Certainly not,' he replied. 'I'm looking to see where I am now!'

At a meeting, to know both where you are and where you are going and to have any resonable hope of arriving, plan your agenda and wherever possible stick to it. Start with: *Apologies for absence.* Who should be there and is not? An absence is often more noticed if an apology is recorded. But non-attenders frequently moan if their apology goes unmentioned. Those present should note who is away.

Next: *Minutes of the previous meeting.* These should have been circulated so that they do not now have to be read. A meeting should refer back before it moves forward.

Next: *Matters arising from the minutes,* not otherwise covered in the agenda. It is usually better to have these dealt with under the (inevitable) final item: *Any other business* (AOB). This hideous heading should be left for the leftovers and not used as an excuse for omitting items which should be discussed, in the hope that no one will raise them, or the end of the meeting may be drawn out in irritation or anger.

Then sort out the guts . . . the body of the discussion. What is the purpose of the meeting? What items do you want laid before it, and which will concern others?

Once you know the topics, move them carefully into order. The layout of the agenda . . . the ordering of the business . . . the selection of items for debate at their appropriate times . . . herein lies the first source of power for the meeting's organisers. If properly carried out, it may do more to flatten opposition and to win the meeting than any other gambit. Here, then, are some of the alternatives, for your cunning consideration:

● Do you put the contentious items at the beginning or at the end? Can you reasonably hope to get them out of the way before your opponents arrive – or after they leave? They can scarcely blame you if they do not turn up on time or if they have to quit before the final whistle – or can they and will they?

● Do you throw up the arguments into the winds of dispute, so that all participants may have a hearty blow, in the hope that when everyone's lungs are wearied, the storm will subside? Or can you hope to sow the wind with such speed and subtlety that you never reap the whirlwind?

● Do you 'get rid of the easy matters first', leaving the battle for the end – by which time (you hope) the meeting will be anxious to conclude, as desk, food or golf course beckon? 'I can stay here all night,' lies the chairperson. 'If you want to go on arguing, that's entirely a matter for you . . .' Will they then conclude – and if so, by doing what you want? Or are you simply asking for a postponement of an hour which will be even more evil when it arrives than it would be if (to remix the metaphors) you grasp the nettle now?

● Should you put the irritation onto the agenda at all –

or hope that the subject may go unnoticed? Recognising the (above referred to) potential horrors of 'AOB', can you reasonably hope that the misery will depart unmentioned?

Human targets for terrorists know that their best defence lies in varying their routes. One renowned royal survivor of a series of assassination attempts credits his continued life to his erratic timekeeping and unpredictable movements. So when plotting the course of your meeting and the downfall of your opponents, look back at the past and this time try another trail. Or perhaps you can rely upon having until now always followed the same agenda – so will a quick switch of tactic trip up those who would kill off your proposals?

Still: The best meetings leave participants satisfied that they have been heard. Loss of cause and of face should not be synonymous. The best track between two points is generally a straight line.

Like the chef preparing ingredients before cooking the meal, the meeting maker sorts out the raw materials, the courses and the menu before throwing the morsels and the chairperson to the lions.

Skilled public speakers sort out ideas in the mind and notes on cards and then shuffle them into an intelligent and logical order which may change during the performance, but which gives strucutre to oratory. No skeleton means no body. Flesh cannot stand alone.

In the same way, no satisfactory meeting can be created or survive without an agenda. The wings of an aircraft flex in a storm or they will crack. A good agenda will retain flexibility. *No* agenda spells only the fair certainty of a meeting crashed into a pile of useless words.

A meeting has been defined as a gathering of people who singly can do nothing, but together can decide that nothing can be done. No agenda means that nothing will be done. If the pressures of life make it impossible to spare the time to prepare the agenda, better to call off the meeting. If virtue is the constant struggle against the law of nature, then holding a meeting without preparing an agenda is vice at its laziest.

14 Minutes

Careful minutes save hours. Careless or non-existent minutes cause as much chaos and confusion in the company or organisation as the Bible tells us existed before the world was created, and almost always at least as much as before the meeting was held. Minutes are the records of the gathering and their taking and checking approval should be as much in the routine of a meeting as its agenda.

Question 1: WHAT should go into the minutes?

Some meetings record and minute every pearl that drops from the lips of each participant. Get the words or the meaning wrong and there will be no forgiveness for your sin. Even if we lose our case, we like to have its essence recorded with due accuracy. Even if our contribution is worthless in the ears of others, its record is important in our eyes, when enshrined on paper.

Unless your meeting has parliamentary importance, in which case, your secretary or recording apparatus will produce your corporate Hansard, the fewer words go into the minutes, the greater good will come out of them. If brevity is the soul of wit, it is the wisdom of the meeting's record.

In general and provided that you do not tread on the pride of too many who are too important, my advice is: Dump the garbage. Forget the arguments – successful or otherwise. Concentrate on conclusions.

Morgan is alleged to have said to his girl friend: 'Gwyneth – your knickers are coming down.'

Gwyneth inspected her apparel and retorted: 'No, they're not, Morgan.'

'Yes they are, my girl,' said Morgan. 'I have decided!'

Minutes should record decisions... conclusions... agreements... Apart from the waste of time, energy and paper in the recording of controversy, its effect is often to reopen the wounds which the decision or agreement was intended to suture. What the participants and those to whom they must report need to know is: What was decided?

Question 2: WHEN do you minute?

As soon as possible. If there is likely to be any argument over the precise detail of that decision, the minute should be made before the meeting even breaks up and signed or initialled by the people responsible. Write it down... read it out... and then demand clear and provable evidence of matters resolved – or, to use the common term, of the resolutions passed.

The United Nations once passed a Resolution on the Middle East, numbered 242. Abba Eban said that Resolution 242 only had one real advantage – it read the same when inscribed from left to right, in English, as it did from right to left, in Hebrew or Arabic. But as the English and the French translations are profoundly different, the parties were left to interpret its meaning as they see fit, or as they can persuade others to see unfit, and implementation is left to the great conquest of Camp David or to the bitter argument of the bullet.

In the more ordinary disputes of industrial relations, an agreement is often arrived at as dawn breaks. Thankfully the management team departs. When its members arrive back later in the morning, they are greeted by a workforce satisfied by what their representatives and leaders genuinely believe to be the agreement – which is probably not the same as the recollection of management. The bargaining begins again and is doubly difficult because mistrust compounds irritation and increases the distance between the parties.

Patience has been described as a minor form of despair, disguised as a virtue. To avoid despair at its most wretched – re-arguing, rediscussing and reviving old disputes – the extra patience required to set out and to accept minutes of agreement is a virtue of some significance.

Hurry is a visible sign of worry, so if the occasion is less anxious and the minute less crucial, it may be made later. Worry is, as Dean Inge proclaimed, 'the interest paid on trouble before it falls due'. You can often avoid both, by making and agreeing your minutes.

Question 3: WHO checks the minutes?

Whoever will take the blame if they are incorrect.

In a decent system – which means one that is as much like our own as possible – the civil servants or other officers or employees, from department head to secretary, may carry the private can. But it is their bosses who must defend them publicly and if necessary resign in the face of disaster. So the compiler of the minute should give the boss the chance to check if he wishes. If he is too busy or too lazy, then he will be as responsible in reality and in morality as he should be in politics, organisational, commercial or corporate.

Usually, the responsible person is the one who was in the chair. If he does not check the minutes, then he should be prepared to explain why.

Question 4: TO WHOM are the minutes CIRCULATED?

To anyone who needs to know their contents.

This normally means anyone who was at the meeting and so took part in the decision-making process, together with anyone else who will be expected to act upon them, and (especially) will be criticised for failure to do so.

Famous last words, as executive departs, defeated: 'Well, Charles, it was in the minutes...' Once those minutes have gone the rounds, anyone who could and should have read them but did not do so has no one else to blame.

Question 5: HOW are minutes CORRECTED?

That depends on your system. In many organisations once the minutes have been circulated, an objector has to raise complaint at the meeting where the minutes are to be confirmed. In others, a word with the Company Secretary or other custodian of the records is enough to have the wrong righted.

The larger the meeting, the more important it becomes to emphasise to participants that suggested corrections should be submitted in advance. If they come your way, read and re-read them, especially if they would change the effect of decisions. Minute changing is a common and successful method of back door revisionism.

If someone asks for a correction, there are then three alternatives: To accept that the original minute was wrong and to alter it; to insist that it was correct and to refuse any alteration; or to negotiate an acceptable form of words. Jaw being better than war, negotiation should not normally follow rejection.

At the start of the next meeting, Item 2 of the agenda will normally be: 'Minutes of previous meeting' (see the last chapter). Any arguments are then resolved, if necessary by re-consideration.

Then there may be 'matters arising from the minutes' (see the last chapter) not dealt with elsewhere on the agenda. These should be few and unimportant. Major decisions should be back on the table, so that the participants can decide whether or not they have been carried into effect and if so with what result and if not then why not.

'Minutes of the last meeting have been circulated,' says the chairperson. 'May I sign them as a correct record? Thank you.' That should be the end of the matter.

Otherwise, objections are considered and discussed, ac-

cepted, modified or rejected – which is time ill spent. Watch
the minutes and your hours will take better care of themselves.

Minute writers have too much power because too few
will bother to read their work and still fewer to correct errors.
Even those who spot what they believe to be mistakes are
chary of corrections, in case they have been tricked by
memory.

It follows that if you wish quiet control over the decision-
making process, you should offer to write – or, if that is
done by the Secretary, to check – the minutes. Keep your
own careful notes; get your drafts cleared by necessary colleagues; then present the minutes to the meeting. You will
win.

Similar principles apply to the preparation of almost
any other type of meeting document. If you are prepared
to 'write a paper' or to 'send out the pros and cons in writing'
or to 'knock the proposal into shape and bring it back next
week', your busy colleagues will be grateful. It may be your
business to ensure that their gratitude is misplaced. Not that
you would twist the meaning of the meeting – but it's not
what you state but the way you state it . . .

Minutes are a record of what happened. You have no
right to re-write the record because conclusions do not suit
you. So (seriously) if you do write the minutes, take care
not to mislead – or certainly not to be caught cheating. Otherwise you will lose the trust of your colleagues and that is
beyond both worth and recall.

On the other hand, no participant can complain if minutes
contain decisions, resolutions or other material which they
dislike. A minute is simply a summary of what actually
occurred.

15 Rules and Order

The law lays down some of the basic rules for the conduct of meetings by limited companies and by public authorities. In all other cases, and in all circumstances not prescribed by law, each organisation may create and follow its own rules. These are usually based on those of the House of Commons. They tend to vary little as between different organisations or societies; and in most bodies they are formalised into 'standing orders'.

Rules for the guidance of both Chair and participants avoid unnecessary disputes over what is or is not the appropriate or customary procedure. It is wise and sensible in any body of size and of substance to lay down rules to govern conduct of its business. This code of practice is usually called 'standing orders' and it sets out details of the conduct of meetings.

Standing orders will generally contain procedures for their own amendment – usually at an annual meeting and by a majority of two thirds or three quarters. Most standing orders also provide that they may be 'suspended', usually by a two-thirds majority of those voting. For instance: standing orders may require a meeting to end at a specified time. If the business is unfinished by that time and it is to continue, then standing orders must be suspended.

Or perhaps there is some matter which should be discussed but is not on the agenda and which is so urgent that it should not wait for 'any other business' – a heading which may itself not be reached.

Someone from the meeting or from the chair will move 'suspension of standing orders'. If the proposal is to be discussed, then so be it. But it may be put straight to the vote.

'Martin Brown has moved suspension of standing orders so that we can discuss ... Those in favour, please show ... Anyone against?'

In the case of a conference with a mass of motions, resolutions and amendments, a 'Standing Orders Committee' should be formed, to move the misery of detailed discussion of agenda and timing away from the conference itself. The Committee will recommend ... the conference will decide ... and the chairman of the Standing Orders Committee will generally respond to the discussion and try to placate those who regard their own pet subject as improperly excluded, taken too late in the day or otherwise given insufficient time or prominence.

16 Points of Order and of Information

All meetings either do or should operate in accordance with rules. If there is no order, there is disorder, which in its turn vitiates the purpose of the gathering. The Chair must therefore keep order. But participants are entitled to expect that the Chair will enforce the rules. Hence 'points of order'.

A 'point of order' is a point raised by a participant to question or challenge the conduct of the meeting. 'On a point of order . . . is it in order for . . .? Surely it cannot be in order that . . . Please may we have your ruling as to whether or not it is in order for . . .'

The Chair then rules as to whether or not the point is a good one. The rules of the organisation – often contained in its 'standing orders' – should then be followed. They may also provide the means for challenge of a ruling from the Chair.

In most organisations, points of order have priority. They may be raised at any time, except when the person in the chair is actually speaking or calling for order. As a result, a 'point or order' may in practice be a point of disorder.

In Parliament and elsewhere, points of order are frequently misused, as methods of disruption or of delay. It is then for the Chair to respond with such firmness as is appropriate. The skill, fairness and expertise of the Chair – or their absence – are then clearly revealed.

If you have to deal with disorderly points of order, here are some suggestions:

● Get the meeting on your side. If someone is really being difficult, get neighbours to wave down the interrupter: 'Oh, come on . . . let's get on with the agenda . . .'

● Keep calm. Lose your cool and you lose your point.

● Even though you may be bound to take a point of order, you may say: 'I will take that point of order at the end of this speech . . . Please allow Mrs Brown to finish . . . Let's get on with the business and deal with that point of order a little later . . .'

● If the point is genuine and you have got something wrong, then say so: 'That is a fair point. So let us now . . .' Or: 'Would it not be the wish of the meeting that we get on with this item, although strictly speaking perhaps we should not . . .?'

● Rule with firmness – and hope for the best. 'I am bound to make a ruling. I think that there is some doubt about it, but I believe that it would be best for us all if we . . .' Or even: 'I would be most grateful if we could now get on with the business. But my ruling is . . . If anyone does wish to dispute it, then of course they may. But . . .'

If you run into the interruption which is not a point of order at all but merely a means of destroying someone else's speech or making an unwarranted disruption or intervention, firmness is vital. 'That is not a point of order . . .' Or: 'As Mr Green well knows, that is not a matter for the Chair . . .' The Chair is in charge of order but does not decide on matters of debate or discussion. It is for the participants to put their own points of view and not for the Chair to rule any viewpoint out of order – unless it is. It could be because:

● it is defamatory

● it raises points which are themselves out of order – perhaps because they do not come under the particular item

under the agenda but should be raised later, perhaps
because they have already been decided at that meeting
or within a prescribed time limit and should not now
be raised at all.

● it involves an improper attack on the Chair, on another
colleague or on a third party.

A point of order, then, must concern the order of the
meeting. It must not be permitted to strangle discussion or
to prevent someone from expressing a viewpoint, however
unpopular. As every Speaker in the Commons has to say,
too often: 'The Honourable Member is entitled to put his
point...' Or: 'That is not a Point of Order. It is an abuse
of the procedures of the House... As the Honourable Lady
well knows, that is a matter for the Government (*or as the
case may be*) – and certainly not for the Chair.'

Points of order are sometimes used by those wishing
to respond to personal attack. Some organisations allow
'points of personal explanation', but the purpose is clear and
proper. Someone who has, in his or her own view or in
reality or both, suffered from an unfair attack should be
allowed to respond. One of the top jobs of the Chair should
be to protect people against personal abuse.

In the House, attacks on individuals are as much part
of the cut and thrust of debate as assaults on ideas, provided
that the prescribed marks are not overstepped.

You may not accuse a colleague of telling a lie. When
Mr Speaker called Sir Winston Churchill to order for accus-
ing someone of telling a lie, he withdrew rapidly: 'I apologise,
Mr Speaker,' he said. 'Let us call it simply a terminological
inexactitude!' You may properly accuse someone of error
but not of deliberate untruth.

I once presided over a meeting at which a colleague
saw fit to make a remark which I regarded as offensive to
black people. I asked him to stop. Instead, he resigned from
the organisation. That was his loss, not ours.

I asked Lord (Manny) Shinwell whether it was true
that he had threatened to resign if the Government in which
he was Minister of War did not take a certain step which

he regarded as essential. 'Certainly not, my boy,' he retorted. 'I have neither resigned nor threatened to resign nor would I. If you do you lose!'

So if you are in the chair and are yourself pulled up on a proper point of order, admit your error. Neither resign nor threaten to do so or you will lose not only the hour but also the day and the case.

Which leaves: 'points of information'. These are a menace and should not be permitted by standing orders or other rules or by the Chair. 'On a point of information, Mr Chairman, may I tell the meeting that...' No. You are trying to jump the queue. Please wait until it is your turn to speak. 'On a point of information, is Mr White not aware that...' If he is not, then yours is no way to inform him...

In practice, whether or not the Chair permits an interruption in the guise of a point of order or any other is a matter of discretion, to be exercised with common sense. As for the participant wishing to do the interrupting: The art may be summed up thus:

● Address the Chair and put your point of order in appropriate form:

'On a point of order, Mr Chairman, may I have an answer to my question?'

'Is it in order for Mr Gold to speak at this stage? Surely the question of... should be left to item 8 on the agenda?'...

'On a point of order and through the Chair, may I appeal to colleagues not to...'

'On a point of order, would it not be better to refer this unhappy matter to a subcommittee? Perhaps I could suggest that it consist of...'

● Be firm in your 'I am entitled to ask a point of order...' – but do not persist beyond the patience of the meeting. Watch for shaking heads, clucking tongues or signs of irritation. Unless your purpose is specifically to destroy the meeting, do not set it against you through blatant abuse of procedures.

● In Parliament points of order are frequently used as

instruments of delay, to avert or put off evil hours or
nasty subjects. It is the duty of the Opposition to oppose
and procedural methods are, within democratic limits,
both inevitable and proper. You exceed those limits at
your meeting at the peril of your own case and credibility,
as well as that of the meeting.

Finally: Every procedure permits points of order which are
valid. The most important:

● No quorum – rules stipulate that a prescribed number
of members or delegates must be present; they are not;
the meeting can continue unless and until someone calls
attention to the defect, which is generally done on a
point of order; at which stage, if a quorum cannot be
rallied, the meeting may not continue with its business.

● *Ultra vires* – the matter under discussion is 'beyond
the powers' of the body – outside its scope and dealing
with matters which are (for instance) beyond the terms
of reference of the particular committee or not within
the constitution of the body concerned.

● Improper language – although the bounds of 'propriety'
are admirably flexible.

● No question before the meeting – in other words: 'Surely
a specific question should be formulated so that we know
upon what we are expected to decide?' 'This is not on
the agenda and therefore not appropriate to discuss at
this stage.'

Linked with this one, the last,

● Points raised irrelevant to item under discussion – therefore not in order at the present stage and should
(perhaps) be raised under 'any other business' or under
a different agenda item – or maybe next time – or even
never?

17 Resolutions, Motions and Amendments

When a meeting resolves on action or policy, it may do so in the form of a 'resolution'. When someone moves that the meeting adopt a concept or a decision, the 'mover' may propose a 'motion'. Either way, the meeting is invited to concentrate its mind and, if appropriate, to vote on an issue, set out in someone's words.

For the motion or resolution to be in order, it may have to be on the agenda, with due notice given so that those who disagree may know, attend and oppose. It may or may not be proper to put an 'emergency resolution', where it would have been impracticable to give notice. All depends on the rules, procedures or 'standing orders' of the company or other organisation concerned.

Assuming that it is in order to put the proposal before the meeting, the Chair will permit the mover to do so – and (again by rule or perhaps by custom) a time limit will be set. Next: Someone will second the motion. If there are not two people prepared – formally or informally – to support the motion, it will fall.

'The motion is in the name of Mr Brown. He has five minutes to propose it...' Then: 'Thank you, Mr Brown. Do we have a seconder? Miss Green? Do you wish to speak or do you second formally?' If speak she will, then: 'Very well. You have three minutes...'

Then comes the right to oppose. 'Who wishes to speak

against the resolution? Mr White, you wish to oppose? Very well. You have five minutes...' Then: 'Does anyone else wish to speak against the motion?' The opposition should have the same air space as the movers.

Then: 'Does anyone else wish to speak? Mr Gold? Are you in favour or against? In favour? Fine. Please go ahead.'

Then someone on the other side. To be fair in the chair, you balance the debate. This may be easy if you know the people and their views, but the larger the audience, and the more uncertain the view, the harder your task. By all means ask: 'On which side do you wish to speak, madam?' Or: 'I shall now call someone in favour of the proposition – are you for the resolution, sir?'

'I am not decided...'

'Then please give us the benefit of your indecision!' The more bitter the debate, the greater should be your cool, calm and good humour.

Insist that the meeting respects the chair. This process begins by addressing remarks to you. Parliamentary tradition keeps opponents at tongue's length from each other.

'Please address the chair,' you say. 'Through you, Chairman,' responds the speaker, 'I would ask Mr Green to give better reasons for his view than he has.' That is in order.

'That's rubbish, Mr Green,' is not.

If the speeches subside of their own accord, then you call on the proposer to respond to the debate. If time moves faster than tongues, you could say: 'The arguments have been well ventilated. I propose calling one more speaker on each side...' If the suggestion is not greeted with protests, follow it.

Or someone may 'move the closure'. Then enquire: 'Shall we close the debate now?' Or, if appropriate, put it to the vote. 'Those in favour of the closure, please show... Those against?' If people have had enough, the closure will be passed and you call the proposer. If a majority wish the debate to continue, so be it – in the chair you are in the hands of the meeting.

If time is the enemy, remind the audience: 'We have to finish by ten... We must be out of the room... There is another meeting after ours... We have only another half an hour... So shall we discuss this matter for the rest of our time or would you not prefer to come to a decision? It's a matter for you...'

You must always try to give people the feeling that all points of view have had a fair hearing. You may be forced to strangle a debate. The balance between freedom of speech and the calls of nature, home and other business is not always easy to strike. Try you must.

Naturally, however you handle debate and time, you are sure to be criticised. The best way to avoid most criticism but to deserve it most is to do least!

Anyway: Eventually, the debate must end. The resolution or motion is put to the meeting. The vote is taken.

The roads to ruin, deceit and disaster are all paved with good resolutions – and with many bad ones. There are ways to avoid, or at least to mitigate, the misery.

Ban resolutions and amendments where you can. If this proves impossible, impractical or unacceptable, whether for democratic reasons or any other, then try to restrict their number or at least the time spent on their discussion.

Resolutions do have one great advantage, which should be exploited. They force participants to focus their ideas and to concentrate their minds on specific wording, to make a decision and to reach a conclusion, rather than (as one long-suffering chairman puts it) 'drivelling on'. 'If you want to go on with this discussion,' he says, 'then how about putting down a resolution? If you don't want to do that, then I propose moving on...'

By the rules, conventions or wishes of the meeting, resolutions may have to be written... notice may be required... people may need time to think about it... In which case, the respite may enable the argument to be sorted out behind the scenes or, in Parliamentary language, 'through the usual channels'.

If the resolution is in order, then it goes through the usual and proper procedures, but even these may be circumvented. 'Well, Mr Brown, you have already put the arguments in favour of the motion and Miss Patel has supported it. We've had several speeches against. Perhaps we can take a vote at once...?'

If resolutions cannot be avoided, they should be delayed, despatched or otherwise dealt with, with due debate and minimal ill-will.

Amendments present the trickiest challenge for the Chair. The resolution or motion may be altered so as to make it the more – or the less – acceptable ... to soften or to destroy its impact.

A resolution or motion cannot be amended until there is something to amend. So any attempt to move an amendment before the motion itself has been proposed and seconded – and, usually, until any opposition to it has been (as Americans say) 'recognised' – is out of order. If it is clear that the motion is unclear, that it is in the interests and with the consent of the meeting that the motion be amended forthwith, then so be it. Otherwise: Sufficient unto the day be the amendment thereof – a day, if you are lucky, may not arise.

If it does, then the procedure begins again – a debate within a debate. First, the proposer of the amendment, then, formally or by speech, a seconder; then, unless the motion is apparently acceptable to all or at least to most, two people to speak against.

When voting time arrives, the amendment is put first. If it is passed, the meeting votes on the resolution, as amended; if it fails, the original motion is put.

Problems usually arise when the meeting produces a multiplicity of amendments. The same procedures should be followed with each, and if necessary, votes taken in some sensible order.

Procedural wrangles over amendments are too common and too complex. Wise organisers and chairpersons do their best to sort out their miseries, privately and either before or after the meeting.

18 Voting

In a democracy – national, local or organisational – the ultimate way to resolve a difference is to have a vote. That gives those present three choices. They may vote in favour, or against, or they may abstain. Other than in special cases where specific majorities are required – usually by the constitution (e.g. two thirds or three quarters for a change in the constitution itself) – a simple majority will decide.

The chairperson usually has the same right to vote as everyone else, but frequently declines to use it, preferring to remain at least apparently impartial. That is a matter for the Chair. In the case of a tie, the chairperson usually has a casting vote. Again: This does not have to be used.

In practice, persistent critics of the decision taken may seek its overthrow at a future meeting, with their troops duly 'whipped' into the fray. Whether another vote is permissible or permitted depends upon the rules of the organisation and the strength, firmness and views of the Chair.

There are two main methods of voting: the raising and counting of hands – voting by show of hands; and 'secret ballot' – the recording of votes on paper. In most organisations and on most issues, a show of hands is sufficient to indicate the feeling of the meeting.

Secret ballots have both advantages and disadvantages.

In Parliament, all votes are open. Electors, parties and colleagues alike are entitled to know whether and how we vote
on each issue. Secret ballots avoid improper pressures but
mean that your opponents can knock you down in indecent
privacy. The smaller the meeting and the less important the
issue, the less worthwhile it becomes to endure the delay
and bother of written ballotting. Conversely: The more crucial it is and the larger the meeting, the more likely the
need for the ballot box.

Whether or not the Chair calls for a ballot will often
depend upon the rules of the organisation. Often, you can
start with a show of hands and then, if the result is close,
someone may (properly or otherwise) call for a ballot. This
in its turn may be on the basis of one person, one vote.
In some organisations, though, delegates on a card vote will
vote for their section or organisation or union which may
carry votes according to its membership (real or 'paid up'
or affiliated).

If a ballot is a possibility, prepare for it. Assuming that
it is to be held at the meeting, ensure that ballot papers
will be available, either suitably marked off or available for
marking. If there are to be several votes, it helps to distinguish
between them by providing papers of different colours.

Remember to appoint 'tellers'. Impartial and respected
people should do the counting, and preferably not vote on
the issue themselves. Provide them with sheets of paper,
where necessary pre-prepared, for recording the vote.

If hands are to be counted, this may be done from the
chair. In larger meetings, though, officials of the organisation
or impartial tellers should be appointed.

The Chair announces the result. On a show of hands,
it is often enough to say: 'I declare the motion passed –
by a substantial majority.' Or: 'It is clear that the resolution
has failed to secure the necessary two-thirds majority.' Or:
'The result is very close and I would ask you to keep your
hands raised so that we can have a recount.' Or: 'The result
is so close that I think we had better take a ballot. I shall
ask the Secretary to pass round ballot papers.'

Many organisations avoid the embarrassment of
announcing details of elections. The Chair says who has been

elected but does not give the votes. Others provide numbers. As usual, precedent is the best guide to the Chair. 'We have always announced only the names of the winners and never the votes and I propose to adhere to tradition', or: 'It has never been our custom to give details of results, and I do not propose to do so now.'

Naturally, someone may object. That is the privilege of the free. The power of precedent as a guide to conduct – in ballot or in battle – cannot be overstressed. Human beings like the security of the well trodden path. The chairperson in doubt should follow it with determination and leave it only with care. Minefields lie alongside.

Recounts. They are harrowing.

In the 1983 General Election, my colleague and friend Jim Marshall was beaten by 7 votes out of about 65,000 and after five recounts.

Earlier, I had watched the votes piled on my table and that of my opponent mounting up with apparent equality. At one stage I was sure that I was out. 'I've had it,' I muttered to my friend Lawrie Simpkin, Executive Editor of the local paper. 'You're just in,' he replied. 'But only just . . .' He was right. I was in by 1700 and Jim was out by 7. Votes are democratic and fascinating for the observer. They are a trial and a misery for the participants. So be kind to them if they lose.

Most company meetings are ruled by consensus. The chairman (and how many women are there in *those* chairs?) asks his colleagues for their view . . . gets the feel of the meeting . . . then pronounces sentence on the proposal. 'I think we have a consensus that . . ., haven't we?' In the absence of protest, the matter is decided.

Someone may intervene: 'I am sorry, Chairman. I cannot agree. There are too many of us who believe that the proposal would harm the company.'

Then the debate continues or the chairman says: 'Very well. Let us defer the matter until our next meeting," or 'I'll talk about it again with Miss Brown and come back to you at our next meeting,' or 'Let's pass it to a subcommittee. Bill, John and Mary – please report back to us,' or 'I'm sorry, but in that case I shall have to take the decision on my responsibility. I rule that . . .' Subject to a vote of no confidence in the Chair, according to the Rules, if there are any, the matter is thus decided by dictatorial decree.

In trade union meetings, voting is the almost invariable rule. 'Are we all agreed? Those in favour please show. It's unanimous . . .' Or: 'Those in favour, please? Those against? I declare the motion carried by . . .' The voting is stated, recorded, minuted and everyone knows how he or she stands, provided always that the motion or resolution is itself clear and explicable.

Special votes decide specific matters according to rules of company or organisation. Changes in the constitution or in the rules themselves, for instance, must generally be passed by a two-thirds or three-quarters majority – but is it of those present and voting or of the membership?

Again: Voting is usually by a show of hands, but written rules or usual custom may require a secret ballot, either at the meeting or by post. Check the rules.

Anyway: Once the mover of the motion has replied, there is no further discussion. The vote is normally taken . . . the question is 'put' . . . and the matter is decided.

What if there is a tie? In most organisations, the chairman has a vote – which (as discussed at the start of this chapter) he or she may or may not use – plus a casting vote.

If you are in the chair, you may prefer not to take the responsibility of making the final choice. Usually, though, you should. Right or wrong, the meeting must come to a conclusion, on the issue and as a whole. You have been elected chief cook in order to preside over the occasion. When your colleagues cannot agree on the recipe, the decision is yours. And as President Harry Truman remarked in a situation not entirely different: 'If you don't like the heat, get out of the kitchen.'

Still: If you are not forbidden to do so by your standing orders, you may fend off your responsibility – or nudge the meeting in the direction of your choice:

● By saying: 'We have an equal division of opinion. As this matter involves . . . I would prefer not to have to use my casting vote. So let me put the motion again

– just to see if anyone has suffered a change of mind
or, in these circumstances, would prefer to abstain . . .?'

● By putting your own point of view: 'I had not wanted
to come down on one side or the other, but in view
of the equal division of opinion, perhaps I could tell
you how I feel . . . and see whether that might possibly
affect the vote . . .' Or:

● By adjourning the subject to a committee or the motion
to the next meeting – at which (you would doubtless
hope) you could rally your own forces rather better than
you succeeded in doing at this one.

19 Guest Speakers

Family are those whom you may offend without serious risk. They were born into the problems of the tribe. They may keep their distance, but they cannot opt out of membership. Guests – and especially guest speakers – are generally sought after, invited and entirely free to return or not, depending upon their welcome. 'Family hold back' is acceptable. 'Guests do without' is not. So dealing with guests at meetings requires skill and forethought.

First: Whom do you invite – and how many?

Not long ago, the French Director of an international organisation showed me the proposed agenda for a conference of some 200 delegates from 21 countries, over which I was due to preside. At some sessions of only $1\frac{1}{2}$ hours there were listed: Chairman, greetings; addresses; and 'rapporteurs' – average four eminent speakers per session.

I protested. My colleague replied: 'Do not worry. They are not speakers, only "invités". They have only been invited. If we get one in three who accepts, we shall be lucky.' He was wrong. So apparently important was the meeting that no one refused! Result: A parade of the stars . . . a galaxy of set speeches . . . and a conference at which there was no time for anyone to confer.

So we had a conference which was a fine public relations exercise. For the delegates, it was a pain in the ear. As President, the responsibility was mine. It was not made easier to shoulder by the absence of the Director, due to a sad but timely bereavement.

On the first and impressive opening session, which, in continental fashion, was due to begin at the awful hour of 9 in the evening, and actually kicked off quite promptly at about 9.20, we had no less than ten speakers, including the President and Secretary of the European Parliament... one Ambassador and three Ministers... international leaders of mighty stature... plus a choir of forty-five voices from Rumania.

What to do? First: Not to permit any extra speakers. The (extremely distinguished) leader of a (very) important delegation asked for 'just a couple of minutes, please' to deliver a brief message from his sovereign. Against the advice of one of our top executives, I thought: 'What the hell – it's worth two minutes.' I agreed. Result: A ten-minute speech and no message from the sovereign. Never again...

Second: I resolved on supreme self-sacrifice – no opening message from the chair and only brief, friendly, relaxed and generous words to introduce, thank and link the speakers. No problems, especially as most of the audience were not used to the informal style, but enjoyed it. Mistake: In the great heat of TV lights and a muggy evening and to accentuate the informality I took off my jacket. This was deemed inappropriate.

Third: I leaned on the only speaker from our organisation, as a member of the family, to 'hold back'. Would he not make his speech the following day? No way. He had, after all, travelled from the United States... he had a message from the President of the organisation... and anyway (and do watch out for this one): 'I have already given my text to the press...'

I said: 'Never mind that. Tell them that you are delivering a summary... or half of it tonight and the rest tomorrow... Please,' I begged him, 'please understand the problems...'

As a gentleman, a friend and as organisational 'family', he did. Instead of the twenty minutes planned, he spoke for eight.

The leader of our French delegation was even kinder. A gentle Senator from Paris, he cut his contribution to three minutes. I blessed him then and will remember him – which means according him proper billing and maximum time on some other occasion.

Next: The guests. I asked each in turn to be kind enough to be especially brief. I explained the problems. 'How long will your message be?' I asked. 'Very short... about five minutes,' said both the President and the Secretary General of the European Parliament. I thanked tham warmly for their understanding and good nature. Each stuck to his word and to his time.

The same tactic did not, alas, work with either the Ambassador or the two Ministers from his country. Each said: 'About ten minutes'... each turned the deafest of ears to my plea to cut back... and each exceeded his time.

When the senior Minister was in mid-flow, there occurred one of those natural interruptions which cast unexpected pleasure into many meetings. To the accompaniment of a massive thunderclap, the lights went out! An engineer rushed over in the gloom. 'Do not worry, Monsieur,' he said, 'the emergency lighting will be on shortly.'

I thanked the speaker for his words which I suggested had now come to their natural conclusion... and I asked the choir to come into the arena to brighten our darkness. Then, with a blinding flash, on went the lights – and on went the speaker! No hint, natural or supernatural, would suffice to interrupt his message. Nor would the fact that it differed little from those presented by his Ministerial and Ambassadorial colleagues... Some of his audience switched on and others switched off their instantaneous translation machines, along with their minds.

Then came the keynote speaker – that admired and courageous survivor of the holocaust and now author and lawyer of international distinction, Samuel Pisar. Allotted time: 20 minutes. He spoke, with brilliance and restrained passion, for nineteen. Thanks to him and to a glorious performance by our young choir, the evening survived its *embarras de richesses* – that superabundance of speakers which we should never have had to endure.

The same, alas, could not be said of much of the rest of the conference. Each session was overburdened with talent. Of discussion and debate there was none.

First rule on inviting guests: Invite few, that your blessings may be many.

Airlines invariably overbook, some 'scientifically' and others uncaring. Wise passengers on busy flights arrive early and, if necessary, 'pull rank' – scream their way into available places. Result: For those offloaded, misery, and for the airline, ill-will which money may repair.

Planning a dinner party – public or private, at home or at business? Then you, too, may count on refusals. But do not overcount or you may have to offload.

As with dinners, so with meetings. Mind whom you ask and resist the temptation to over-invite. Remember Strasbourg... learn from my mistakes and those of my Director ... we shall!

20 Votes of Thanks

The words 'thank you' can rarely be overused. But most 'votes of thanks' are overdone.

The purpose of a public statement of appreciation should simply be to say 'thank you'. That could conveniently be done from the Chair. In practice, though, the giving of the vote of thanks is too often a privilege conferred on some worthy person as a gesture of goodwill or to fend off offence.

Thus: 'Bill has been upset with us for too long ... let's give him the vote of thanks ...' Or 'Maybe we could shut Mary up by giving her the vote of thanks' or (worse) 'Jack is a pain in the entrails. Let's think – where can he do least harm? I know ... the vote of thanks! Even he can't louse that up for too long ...' Can he not? He will ...

If you must confer a vote of thanks as a posthumous award to the living, so be it. Otherwise, choose:

● A distinguished and articulate person, who will see the task as thanking and honouring the speaker rather than inflating his or her own self-esteem, or

● Someone whom you wish to bring forward, to encourage, to promote – and upon whom you can reasonably rely to do the job; and *not* a speaker who will let you down by self-puffing – who will use the wrong opportunity to make the wrong speech for the wrong length of time.

What, then, if you are the giver of the vote of thanks? How should you handle it?

Do the job: Thank the speaker. Call on the meeting to applaud. Speak with concise sincerity. Then sit down.

The job is to thank the speaker for what has been said. Unless you have been supplied in advance with a copy of the speech, you cannot conceivably thank with sincerity from a prepared text.

'I call on our colleague, Martin Hughes, to propose the vote of thanks.' Polite applause and up gets Mr Hughes, clutching a typewritten sheet, from which he reads as follows, in a monotone and with his eyes down on the paper. 'We all thank our speaker for his wonderful address. It was a pleasure to hear him. He has articulated the views and feelings of us all and has provided an expert focus to our work...' And so on and so on – all of it obviously insincere because it was typewritten before Mr Hughes had heard the speech.

The speaker might have prepared a skeleton and put it onto cards, then the preparation would have been invisible. He might even have followed the suggestion in this book and jotted notes on the cards during the course of the speech.

So avoid the pre-prepared if you can and otherwise hide the pre-preparation. It is bad to read any speech other than the most crucial or complex. It is invariably wicked to read a vote of thanks.

Start by drawing words or ideas straight out of the speech that you have heard. Indicate your interest and your attention. 'Miss Brown has said that...' or 'We have listened with great interest to the account of...' Or 'As Mr Green correctly pointed out...'

As a composer weaves variations upon another's theme so by all means do the speaker the compliment of adding an extra edge to his or her ideas, observations, suggestions, warnings, words...

Perhaps you could lift out of the speech the basic moral which you have found. Or you might take a sentence or even a witticism and add to it. 'That was a very good story about... wasn't it? It reminds me of another tale, here in our own company/organisation... there was that wonderful moment when...'

Repetition of the main theme – variation of your own . . .
a little harmony . . . and you do well.

Do not misuse the occasion for criticism or for attack.
A tactful, modest word of admonition is sometimes possible
– like: 'I was a little sorry that our speaker did not mention
that . . .' Or: 'I am sure that Mr Green will not mind my
mentioning that . . .' Then perhaps make good the omission.
But do it tactfully: Not: 'Green is an idiot, forgetting to
mention that . . .' Rather: 'I am sure that by not mentioning . . . no offence whatever was intended . . .' Or 'the omission
of . . . was, I know, totally unintentional and Roger will not
mind my adding a word in praise of . . .'

Then wind up. Bring your mini-speech to its maxi-climax
– the clap of applause. The vote of thanks is a minor speech
on what may be a major occasion, if not for the gathering,
then at least for the speaker. So structure it like any other.

Introduction: 'Chairman, Roger Green, colleagues and
friends . . .' Then a good opening sentence: 'Mr Green has
said that . . . He was right, wasn't he? How grateful we are
to him for putting into words the main theme of our work,
and for putting our sights onto our targets, which we too
often forget.' Straight in with the thanks.

Then a variation or two – for a minute or two, and
not more. Followed by the summary, wind up, climax. 'So
please join me in thanking Mr Green for his superb and
thoughtful address.'

Do avoid the clichés in the vote of thanks:

● 'We are so grateful to Mr Green for sparing us so much
of his valuable time . . .'

● 'I don't know how Mr Green manages to fit so much
into his time. We do thank him for sparing this evening
for us . . .'

● 'So please put your hands together and give a good clap
for our guest speaker . . .'

● 'We do hope to see our speaker again before long.'

Having thanked the speaker, do not say: 'Thank you'
before you sit down. End on the climax.

'So, Mr Green – many thanks indeed for your address. We shall remember your advice – and do our best to follow it.' Then turn towards the speaker . . . start the clapping yourself . . . the audience will join in . . . Then you sit down, with you job well and briskly done. Your colleagues may not invite the speaker to address them again, but they will be pleased to ask you to do votes of thanks.

21 Question Time

On most days, and especially on Tuesdays and Thursdays, Question Time is the best part of the parliamentary day. Ministers are held to swift account ... back benchers by the dozen vie as prodding critics ... and every ex-Prime-Minister has admitted that the twice-weekly gruelling duelling quarter-hours of Opposition queries and taunts tested the mettle.

A Parliamentary Question is sometimes asked in the hope of getting an illuminating answer, but not often. Usually, its purpose is either to lay bare the (hoped for) ignorance of the Minister or as a bland introduction to a devastating 'supplementary'. For information or for destruction, there is no substitute for a well-barbed query.

A parliamentarian who questions well and answers with distinction earns high regard. Conversely: those who collapse under questions are mocked. A speech allows the speaker to say what he or she wishes to say. Questions give at least a chance to force out what the questioner and the audience wish to hear.

As with the House of Commons, so with houses of business ... and so with meetings of any sort.

Questions need careful handling.

Problem 1 for Chair and speaker alike: When are questions accepted? Should you allow interruptions during the course of the speech or presentation or reserve them for the end?

Again we look to parliamentary precedent and procedure. Do you wish to interrupt? Then it is for the speaker to decide whether or not to give way.

The would-be interrupter stands and gesticulates. 'Will the Rt. Hon. Gentleman give way?'

'With pleasure.'

'I thank the Rt. Hon. Gentleman for his courtesy... But has he not considered... Why does he say that... Surely it is ludicrous to suggest to the House that...?'

Expert speakers give way when it suits them. If they know their case and are unafraid of interruptions, they can usually batter their opposition. After all, they do not actually have to answer the questions asked, and most do not. The art is to appear to answer and to use the interruption to destroy the questioner – assuming, that is, that the query does not come from your own side.

My advice: The more formal, complex or potentially boring your presentation, the more ready you should be to give way to interruptions. Other than in the most formal address, I invite questions – at the right time, which is in a natural break in the argument.

Again: Parliament: 'Will the Honourable Gentleman give way?'

'With pleasure, when I have completed this line of reasoning.'

If you are in command of your audience... you 'have the floor'... then *you* should decide when it suits you and your argument best to allow questions.

How should questions be handled from the chair? That depends mainly on the skill of the speaker and the intent and method of the would-be interrupters.

Expert speakers perfer to deal with their own questioners, interrupters, hecklers. Part of the challenge – and, indeed, of the fun – of presentations is to provoke and then to handle the question.

If a chairman tries to handle my audience, I say: 'Thank you, Chairman – but I am very happy to deal with this question. It shows precisely the weakness in the case put

by our opponents...' Or: 'That's all right, Bob. I'll handle
the question, with pleasure – but if Martin doesn't mind,
I'll do it in a few moments, when I come to that area...'

With an apprehensive speaker, though, the Chair may
have to intervene. 'I am sorry, but I cannot allow questions
at this stage... Please have the courtesy to let Mary Brown
put her point...' Or, as Mr Speaker is wont to chide: 'The
Honourable Member is entitled to put his point of view.'
It is the job of the Chair to ensure freedom of speech at
any meeting.

When to respond to questions is itself a key question.
How to do so is another. The basic rule: Prepare... know
your case... and look out for the chinks in your oratorical
armour.

I once spent a fascinating day with the then UK Ambassador to the United Nations, my friend Ivor Richard, who
later became an EEC Commissioner. At the time he was
in Switzerland, leading the UK effort to resolve the Rhodesia
dispute. He was due to face an (inevitably critical) press
grilling at 12 noon.

From 10.30 to 11.30 I listened while Ivor was put
through the grinder by his own most senior staff. 'Ambassador, why do you say this... Surely that must be wrong...
But, with respect, that leaves the question open about...?'
Together they looked at the questions and worked out the
most appropriate answers.

Every Prime Minister spends useful time considering
the questions that he or she is likely to be asked, and thrashing
out answers. Most of the best impromptu replies, including
brilliant quips, are carefully rehearsed.

If preparation of that sort is good enough for Prime
Ministers and their Ambassadors, it should do for you. Know
your case and you should succeed. Otherwise you will be
lucky if you do not manifestly fail.

National Coal Board Chairman Ian McGregor appeared
before a Parliamentary Select Committee on Employment.
Under the heading: 'Mac gets knifed in a place of strife',
the *Guardian* correspondent described his débâcle:

The young Scottish Labour MP, Gordon Brown... gave

Mr McGregor what must have been one of the roughest 20 minutes he has had to endure, even in the last two trouble-packed years. They hadn't used normal procedure in abnormal, strike bound times; but why hadn't they used them in cases which had arisen since the strike was over? A long – fatal – pause. 'That', said Mr McGregor, 'is an interesting point.'

He never recovered. More and more he had to turn to officials for urgent information or aid. Greville Janner (Lab. Leicester West) who is a real QC (Gordon Brown is only a reformed journalist) pitched in with a barrage of questions he knew the Coal Board Chairman would not be able to answer. ('And please don't consult,' he implored him.) This was not just theatre: It was almost a theatre of cruelty . . .

So it was. Meetings are theatres . . . Speakers are actors, who write their own scripts, and who must expect to be interrupted in their flow . . . The person in the Chair is the producer and director, in charge, but often only just . . . Questioners from the audience have immense potential and power.

The Select Committee, is, of course, an unusual forum which, if you are fortunate, you will not have to face. But the same basic rules apply if you are addressing your own Board or someone else's . . . if you are propounding or defending plans, prospects or proposals . . . if you are selling projects or products, goods, services or ideas.

The set speech has its place on any stage. When it comes to the question . . . the interruption . . . the clash of minds and ideas, subject to the whim and the word of the moment – that is when you recognise the artist at any meeting.

PART III

IN THE CHAIR

22 Winning your Meeting – from the Chair

The object of a meeting is to win. To do so without opposition is a pleasure. But to overcome the opponent or the enemy, that is the truer triumph. To achieve your object and to leave your participants as satisfied as yourself – well, that requires an astute combination of preparation and of patience, of cunning and of good fortune.

Studying criminology at Harvard Law School in the early 1950s, I was shown the electric chair at Sing Sing prison by a macabre and witty warden. He told me of the man who did not like to admit that his father had (as the officer put it) 'been fried'. So he told enquirers that his old man had been 'an academic'. He had 'held the chair of applied electricity at New York State'!

In its own way, the chair of a meeting may be equally lethal. It may at the same moment destroy the effect of the gathering and the reputation of the person in the chair. The art of winning meetings is worthy of careful study.

You could begin by observing the horrors who, with all the subtlety of the animal kingdom, destroy the meetings they chair. You will recognise those who have ears, but who neither listen nor hear... who hold forth without end...

and who leave the participants – around the table, on the platform or on the floor – wondering why they bothered to come. To win at least apparently by consent requires an ear larger than the mouth.

The more difficult the meeting, the greater the need for patience. Let the winds blow. The louder the mouths, the greater the chances that the minds will turn in your direction.

If the opposition becomes too unruly or outrageous, irresponsible or uncontrollable, then try either of two classic moves – or both:

● Adjourn the meeting.

If Speaker George Thomas, now Lord Tonypandy, could not get his way – which meant, an end to turmoil and anger – he would simply adjourn the session. It could be for ten or twenty minutes or overnight. On the principle that you should never argue with an angry man, he would allow the ill humour to subside. Invariably the House returned in more sober and malleable mood.

● Refer the dispute to a committee.

A Parliamentary Committee has been described as a cul-de-sac into which ideas are lured, there to be quietly strangled to death. Many – too many – unwanted ideas have been murdered in that fashion.

Take care, though. A camel has been defined as a horse invented by a committee. Once a camel has been created, it may acquire life of its own. Be sure that your temporary expedient does not turn into an unkillable monster.

So be doubly cautious before you adjourn the meeting and pass the problem to a committee, by whatever name – commission, working party, committee of enquiry or any other. The key to conquest by that route is held by the person in the saddle of the camel – which should either be yourself or (preferably) a trusted and expert colleague.

In preparing to win your meeting, your choice of colleagues is crucial. If you cannot prescribe who takes part in the gathering, then at least ensure that your own side and viewpoint are well represented. Feed your audience with those who will put your case . . . plant your ideas where they will grow from the tongues of others . . . It is not enough yourself to know your case. The greater the opposition, the more you should transfer the burden of argument onto others.

Most importantly, and in the long run, the Chair must at least appear to be fair. Even the executive dictator will do a better job if his colleagues are not in constant fear of losing theirs.

Lenin defined 'the decisive victory of the Revolution over Tsarism' as 'the revolutionary–democratic dictatorship of the proletariat and the peasantry'. That might have been fine for old Lenin, but it should not do for you, in the chair of any meeting of your organisational or corporate peasantry.

The ultimate, though, and the only way always to win in the chair is never to admit that you have lost. If you cannot get your way, shrug: 'If that is the way the meeting wants it, then so be it . . .'

As we saw in Chapter 18, board meetings operate by consensus, trade union gatherings by vote: Those who have the majority with them could learn from the unions.

'I am in your hands. If it is the wish of the meeting that . . . Well, let's see how you feel about it . . .'

At the small meeting, you could ask each of your colleagues for a view. At a large one, why not try a show of hands? Careful, though. Be prepared to lose gracefully. If in doubt, adjourn . . . refer to a committee . . . or call on a cohort to try again to induce the meeting to see reason.

In law, the mythical 'reasonable man' has been defined as 'the man on the Clapham omnibus' – a vehicle which has long since ceased to exist. To win a meeting from the chair means: To convince the participants that your view is that of moderate, reasonable people . . . that to disagree with you is immoderate, unreasonable, and (hopefully) unpopular, unintelligent, unimaginative: in a word, wrong.

Vic Feather, then TUC leader, once said: 'Industrial relations are like sexual relations. It's better between two consenting parties!' As with the bed, so with the chair. Consent counts.

If a meeting is dull, there are two likely culprits – the

person in the chair, and the one on his or her feet, respectively. The former is the more to blame. The speaker should have been given guidance or instructions on time and subject and, insofar as courtesy permits, kept to them.

It should be a principal aim and duty of the Chair to keep meetings as interesting as possible. This may involve:

● Choosing speakers who are likely to please and ignoring those known to bore.

● Exercising strict control of time – and imposing extra limits on those who outrun their listeners' patience, even if they remain within the limits in the rules.

● Punctuating the meeting with exhortation, explanation or wit.

● Preparing meetings so as to include items of likely importance and hence interest and to exclude the rest. Relegation of the unimportant to the end is a useful alternative – relying on the wish of the meeting at that stage to complete its business and conclude.

Remember: If those who attend today's meeting have no interest in proceedings, they will not return for the next one – unless, of course, they have no alternative. Even then, those who lose interest make small contributions.

23 In the Chair

Taking the chair at a meeting is a trial for the uninitiated, a challenge for the expert and a delight to the successful. The techniques need learning. Their basis is the same whether you are steering a meeting of five or fifty, of staff or of workforce, of managers or of managed, of your colleagues or of strangers. Application and style will differ. But like all other skills, that of the chairperson is the same, wherever it is practised.

The Chair sets the tone, the mood and the atmosphere of the meeting. Like the conductor of a bus, the captain of a ship or a military unit, or the head of any organisation, large or small, he or she is responsible for the tone and for the tenor of the kingdom, large or small.

The Chair must either take charge of the preparations or at least check that they have been properly made. He or she must come to the meeting braced for business or battle. Knowing the purpose and how it is to be achieved, the Chair can set the mood.

The Chair takes centre stage, sets up the meeting and welcomes participants. Each should feel welcome. If the gathering is too large for individual words, then at least the Chair should embrace the audience by the sweep of gesture and eye contact. Greet with a smile colleagues who arrive late. Then make them feel that there is purpose in their presence.

'What do you think, John?' 'Have you a view on this, Mary?' Or 'Bill, you've dealt with this sort of problem before. What would you suggest?'

Those in the chair will not merely avoid humiliation – for which they will be seldom forgiven. They will also and especially invite individual involvement.

Use names wherever possible. Write them down, so as not to offend. If your meeting is around a table, put a diagram beside you, with each participant in position and named. Do not rely on memory.

That famous international lawyer, Professor Arthur Goodhart, could never remember names. He used to meet someone whom he knew perfectly well and say, 'My name is Arthur Goodhart. I hope you have not forgotten yours!'

So personalise your audience. In meetings, like elections, every vote may count.

Then: Be fair. You may bestow on the meeting the benefit of your well-considered bias, but if there is to be a debate, do all you can to ensure the balance. Call speakers in turn and on each side. Ensure that all points of view are put. Listen to and protect minorities. In a democracy, it is a citizen's privilege to be wrong. Even if you are running a dictatorship, the art of remaining in power is to create the reality if possible and otherwise at least the illusion that you do so by consent.

Suppose that your ruling is challenged. You want to put an end to a discussion but someone insists on carrying on with it. Say to the meeting: 'It's up to you. I am in your hands. I have plenty of time. But surely both sides have been fully put? What is your wish?'

This tactic brings the audience onto your side. If it does not, then give way gracefully. 'Fine – so let's continue for a while.'

People who come to meetings invariably want to get on with the business, get out of the room, get home to family or golf course. The art is to be brisk, while preserving freedom to speak.

In the chair, patience . . . humour . . . tact . . . a fair mind

– but above all, a cool head – these are your essentials. At the same moment that you lose your cool, you also lose your meeting and your case. However provocative, offensive or unpleasant the attack made on you or yours, preserve your dignity and your calm.

If you allow yourself the luxury of anger, then do so by design and with deliberate calculation. Respect for the Chair is the essence of good order. Those who attend meetings wish them to be ordered. Exception: Those who come to disrupt, and they are best handled by the audience itself.

You may rap with your gavel, tap the table top with your coin or demand silence. But if the person sitting next to the disrupter turns to him and says: 'Belt up!' – in whatever words – then you are not only more likely to achieve your result, but you will also do so by consent.

During a recent doctrinal argument between the Archbishop of Canterbury and the Bishop of Durham, the Archbishop is alleged to have sighed and said to his recalcitrant colleague: 'Well... I suppose there are two points of view on this matter... Yours... and God's!'

If there are two or more points of view at a meeting, it is your task in the chair to see that they are all heard. If the righteous is to prevail, being the one with which you agree, you will keep your audience with you and not by your conduct turn them against the chair.

From the chair, you keep order and conduct the meeting according to its rules or to those of the organisation concerned. Each has its own accepted procedures. Follow them, where you can.

If the rules are complicated, arrange for a respected and well-informed colleague to sit at your side, memory and rule-book at the ready.

Follow the rules when you can and the agenda where convenient. Respect your audience, their views and their time. Adapt your style to your venue and your subject. Then earn for yourself that 'vote of thanks to the chair' with which the courteous meeting should properly conclude.

The true test of a successful gathering comes afterwards. By its results shall it and you be judged. So when the meeting is over, its assessment should begin. The view from the chair should stretch back to planning and preparation and then forward to results and implementation. With techniques put into practice and that practice promoting perfection, you can face the chair of the meeting with assurance. You will harness your own applied electricity to the specific purpose of that gathering.

If you are in the chair, you are in charge. So you take and keep charge. You do not sit like a lump of cheese while the meeting flounders. You do not leave people to call on themselves to speak. In the small meeting, it may be enough to nod in someone's direction. But in most, it is for you to say: 'Michael Brown . . .'

At a larger gathering where people wish to prepare their contribution, if you can sniff out in advance the balance of the debate, you could say: 'Michael Brown, you're next . . . then it will be Janet White . . .'

If you change your mind, then that too will be a decision. 'I'm sorry, Janet – I did promise to call you next. But I think we ought to have someone on the other side of the argument first, if you don't mind . . . So I'll call Jack Black now – and then Janet . . . Mr Black, please.'

Again: If the flow of the meeting is erratic because (perhaps) speakers have to come up to a microphone, it is for you in the chair to say: 'Mr Diamond, you are next. Please come forward and be ready.'

24 Who Speaks?

The greatest single source of power for the Chair is the right to decide who shall have the floor and when and for how long.

There is an ancient Hebrew liturgy, sacred and sanctified and read on the eve of every Yom Kippur – the day when the Book of Life is sealed. The Almighty will then have decided on His programme for the coming year – who shall live and who shall die, who shall be healthy and who shall ail, who shall flourish and who shall wither . . .

The chairperson has a less exalted, less far-reaching and far more restricted role. Still: to decide at a meeting who shall speak and who shall be silent determines the shape, style and effect of the meeting as well as the influence which participants are likely to have upon it. Like all worthwhile powers, and especially those that depend upon the consent of the governed, it must be exercised with discretion, restraint and (again) with a due degree of cunning.

As each topic approaches, jot down those who should obviously speak on it. Start with the proposer or proponent . . . then (perhaps – but certainly if there is a formal resolution or motion) a seconder. Then the prime opponent (again: with someone to second the opposition?). Next: Who will speak 'from the floor' – 'Now then: Who wishes to express a view on this matter?'

Justice (as the Judge said) must not only be done, but be manifestly seen to be done. A debate must be not only balanced but manifestly so.

To win your point may need pre-priming. Who has influence and is likely to be on your side? 'Joe, we have to get this proposal accepted. I know you're in favour. It would be better coming from you than from the chair. Would you please propose it? Fine. Then who would be best to second?'

Try to keep an ally in the wings. 'I think it would be best if I didn't call you at the start, Jane. We'll hold you in reserve and if it looks as if we're having trouble, may I call you then?'

In debate or discussion or at question time, would-be speakers or questioners vie to 'catch your eye'. In the land of the blind, the one-eyed man is king. In the chair of a meeting, the occupant with selective blindness holds sovereign sway.

Nelson clapped his telescope to his blind eye to block out the sight of a signal he did not wish to see. Remember him when you are in the chair. I wish you intelligent blindness to the demands for attention of those who have spoken too long or too often ... for the bores and the 'nudniks' (an expressive Yiddish word, improved when the person has a PhD and becomes a 'Phudnik'!)

To exclude an opponent from the floor is usually unwise, particularly if the attack is to be made on yourself. My system on such occasions is invariable. I invite the attacker to make his point. I give him as much time as he requires. If others protest at this leeway, I retort: 'Mr Brown has criticisms to make of myself. Please allow him the extra courtesy to make them as he sees fit – right or wrong, he is entitled to make his point.' Then you can turn to him and say: 'Perhaps it would be courtesy, Mr Brown, if you could make your point a little more briefly ...'

Charm, cool and courteous – that is the correct response to the critic. To gag the opponent is to endow the argument against you with unwarranted strength. It gives its proponent the sympathy which decent people give to the oppressed.

Conversely: To provide time, floor and courteous attention to those who disagree with you turns opinion towards you, deflects hostility and invites the honourable to say – to themselves and (you may reasonably hope) to the meeting: 'Well, even if a mistake was made, the criticism has been heard – so let's get on with the agenda . . .' You have then successfully retreated the better to leap forward – or as the French say, so much better, the art is 'reculer pour mieux sauter'.

The length of speeches may be laid down in your rules. Usually it is not; then play the debate by ear. If in doubt, ask the meeting. 'We have a lot on our agenda. Shall we give this discussion another ten minutes? Or have we ventilated different viewpoints, so that we can come to a consensus . . . a decision . . . a vote . . .? Or would you like us to use the rest of the meeting for this subject and leave the rest over until next time?'

Too many meetings spend too long in discussing what they are going to discuss and how long they should spend doing it. To meet to discuss meetings is an irritation which should be left to the United Nations, most of whose delegates are at least well paid for their inaction – and if words can avoid wars, they are worth their weight in unshed blood.

Still: Most meetings will appreciate firmness from the Chair. If, but only if, the Chair is fair, most speakers will accept the discipline of imposed brevity.

How, then, do you best interrupt and shorten the length of wind? Here are some suggestions:

● Pass the speaker a note. 'Please be brief.'*

● In the case of a set speech, agree in advance on timing, always allocating the speaker a few minutes less than you require – most orators will overrun. Ask: 'When you come within, say, five minutes from time, shall I give you an indication?' Most speakers will readily agree. Then no offence is caused when you find a pause in the flow and pass a quiet note: 'Five minutes, please.'

● At an informal meeting, wait till the speaker has reached

---

*See also page 20.

what appears to be a break in the argument and say, quietly but firmly: 'I'm sorry, Jean, but I must ask you to conclude . . .' Or: 'Come on, Bill. I've let you overrun your time . . . Can you wind up fairly soon, please?'

● At a formal session, try simply standing up. The speaker may say: 'Just finishing, Harry.' But if your stance goes unnoticed, speak out – into your mike, if you have one: 'I'm sorry. You must finish now.'

● Quietly invite a colleague to interrupt. Pass a note: 'It's going on too long. Can you try to stop him?' Your colleague then says something like this: 'On a point of order, Mr Chairman. We have to finish by six. Surely we must come to a vote?' Or perhaps he tugs at the speaker's jacket: 'Come on, Mary. I've a client coming in five minutes.'

● In even more formal meetings, someone may shout out 'closure'. The Chair may accept the motion to close the discussion or may say: 'Let's give Mr Green another three minutes, shall we?' Or: 'The closure has been called for. Let me take the feeling of the meeting. Those who feel that we have had enough discussion on this matter, please show?' You may wish to give an indication of your own view, but that which is decided by the meeting cannot thereafter be blamed on you. You are not throttling discussion if the meeting applies the garotte.

25 Involving the Audience

Funerals are the only occasion when you talk to the dead. So why do the speaker, the Chair and the platform at so many meetings treat the listeners like an array of corpses? Audience involvement means success at any gathering.

Involvement may be vocal. The key question: 'What do you think?' Then listen. The rubber stamp and the sponge may have their uses, but the smaller the meeting, the greater the need for participation.

Or take questions – during or after the presentation – and decide which (see Chapter 21).

True involvement means: engaging the personal interest of each listener in the speaker's theme and variations. The skilled orator plays on the minds and emotions of the audience, while the Chair orchestrates the harmony or controls the disharmony. Each person at a meeting is part of the orchestra. Involvement begins when the meeting is called to order. No silence, no attention? Then the meeting does not begin.

Rap with the gavel . . . a sharp tap with a coin on a glass or jug and the meeting is called to order. People are still talking? Then do not begin. 'Mr Brown . . . shall we start? Miss Jones, are you ready? Ladies and gentlemen – your attention, please.'

Look at your audience. The smaller the numbers, the easier it is to fix each eye with yours. Eye contact is as vital from the Chair as it is from the speaker.

Even with a large audience, the skilled chairperson watches instinctively for inattention, fidgeting, yawning. The unskilled should deliberately observe the eyes of the audience. If the eyes of the world of the meeting are upon the Chair, then the beholders are involved.

Expert speakers include their audience in precisely the same way. From the start, they cast their eyes on each.

Martin White speaks seated. He sits upright and never slouches – that gives authority. He does not lean forward towards his audience because that appears aggressive. He reserves that gesture for emphasis or remonstration. He demands the attention of his audience and gets it.

Mary Green prefers to speak standing. So do most skilled speakers when given the choice. If you stand and the audience sits, you automatically dominate and command attention. You are upright and relaxed and you do not begin until both you and the audience are ready. You button or unbutton your jacket, whichever makes you more comfortable. (In the House of Commons the division among jacket wearers is about equal.) You adjust your dress, prepare your mind and then wait until the audience is settled.

'Ladies and gentlemen,' says Miss Green. Each of them feels that he or she is individually addressed because the speaker looks at each in turn.

Teaching presentation to a group of executives, I sat at the side of the room. When a speaker had finished, I asked him: 'Why didn't you ever look at me?'

'Because you were at the side.'

'Don't people at the side matter?'

'Yes – but I couldn't have looked at each person on each side and at the centre or I would not have had time left to speak!'

'Rubbish – it takes no more time to sweep your eye across your audience than it does to take soft butter and spread it across hard bread.'

Still: The most vital involvement begins along with the speech, the address, the discourse, the argument. How?

By using the active and avoiding the passive ... by using the personal and avoiding the impersonal ... by attacking the practical and leaving the theoretical ... by making each listener feel that each word is directed at his or her interests.

For instance: I often lecture on the rules on unfair dismissal. Instead of telling people how to deal fairly with others, I point the anxiety at each of them.

Thus: 'I know that you have been sent here at the expense of your company in order to cope better with the procedures of discipline and dismissal, directed at others. But knowing some of you as I do, I shall tell you how to make sure that when *you* are dismissed, *you* will get as much money as possible from *your* employers ...'

'I will tell you when *you* are qualified for unfair dismissal protection and how to get it ... why *you* must wait for one or for two years before the law will help *you*, unless *you* are sacked for sex or race or trade union discrimination ... and why documentation is vital for *you*, if *you* are to look after *your* interests, *your* job, *your* family ...'

The emphasis is on 'you' and 'yours' ... 'You' are personally involved.

Ever since the Israelites escaped from Egypt, Jewish families have celebrated the Passover with a family reading of 'The Haggadah', a book which tells the story of that epic Exodus. We are required to tell our children that it was 'we' who went out of Egypt – 'I and not he ...' It is, if you will forgive the expression, 'I'dentification. We treat the escape personally.

Then, the story is told of the four sons. One is wise, one simple; one does not know how to ask the right question and one is wicked. It is the wicked one who asks: 'What is this to me?'

This ancient tale has its modern application in every meeting. By all means ask yourself in advance: What is the meaning of the subject to the audience? If it has no relevance, then keep off it altogether if you can; otherwise treat it swiftly.

If in doubt, ask. 'Shall we deal with ...? How many of you would like us to start with ...? Michael ... Mary ... Have you any experience of ...? Do you consider it relevant to our company?'

Talking on health and safety at work, I like to begin: 'Which of you has had an accident at work? You are not here for your health, so presumably you are concerned about the safety of others. Has anyone here had to deal recently with a death or serious injury?' If that attack fails, then the next one *must* succeed: 'Well, who has been in or seen an accident on the road?'

Attention follows interest which is best concentrated on personal concerns. 'Who can tell us about the practical implications of these tax measures? Why do you think that the Government has taken this step? Who can suggest the best response to this attack... Is there anyone here who can help...? Please would you indicate? Thank you – Mr Brown...' Or: 'I call on the gentleman at the back...'

If you can convince your audience from the start that you are dealing with 'I' and not 'he', then you will win... If 'you' replaces 'I' as the most important word in your spoken vocabulary, then 'you' and your meeting are unlikely to fail. Your message will overcome the apprehension and the apathy with which most normal people approach most meetings.

26 Your Good Health

The universal MP's greeting, one to the other, is simply: 'How are you?' I once replied: 'Terrible. Extremely ill.' 'Oh good!' nodded my colleague hurrying on his way.

So if anyone asks: 'How are you?' There are generally two good reasons for not replying. First: The enquirer will not be the least interested in your reply. Second: If by any miracle the questioner cares, then any complaint you may make will be held against you.

Thus: 'Well, how are you?'

'No good. I've been under the doctor for the last three weeks . . .' – which is, of course, itself one of the more charming expressions in the English language.

If you have a complaint, keep it to yourself. Reject any invitation to explain.

When Prime Minister Benjamin Disraeli forgot someone's name, he would not say: 'How are you?', and hope that he would not be told. He would simply say: 'Good morning to you – and how is the old complaint?' In return for taking the chance that he would be told, he had avoided offence.

Still: There is much truth in the old Yiddish admonition which (roughly translated) reads: 'Questions are not Kosher'. In other words: If the answer to your question may not be to your liking, do not ask it.

American slang has adapted these words. Thus: 'How are you?' 'Don't ask ...!'

Now transfer these truths, precepts and principles to the handling of meetings. They lead to the following conclusions:

● At the start, by all means commiserate with Mr Brown on the ill health of his wife ... express sadness at the absence of Ms Jones, whom you hope will have a speedy recovery from her operation ... or, more cheerfully, welcome back Mr White, after his bout of gout ... Then move on to the business.

● Do not ask Mr White how he is feeling. The more elderly and ailing he is, the longer his likely answer. A speaker once apologised to Bob Monkhouse for the length of his wind. 'Never mind,' said Monkhouse. 'You have helped to shorten the winter!' So if you want to view the spring from home, when it comes to health – don't ask.

● Exception: If a colleague is obviously anxious because of family illness, then a quiet word before the meeting will be much appreciated. 'You are really interested in item 5 on the agenda ... let's take it first so that you can get back to Mary as soon as possible ...'

   Or you notice that James is looking sick. Pass him a quiet note: 'Would you like us to take item 7 now, so that you can get away and catch up with your sleep? It must have been a rough journey from ...'

● Kindness from the Chair means attention to individual detail – but the quieter the better and the more appreciated.

27 Preparations

The time to win a meeting is before it begins. That means: preparation.

Whether you are haranguing, encouraging or criticising your staff or workforce, your clients or customers, insiders or outsiders... whether you are seeking their involvement, their guidance, their ideas, their sympathy, their co-operation or their cash... you meet for a purpose. Unless you wish to join the mighty ranks of those who meet wholly or partly in vain – prepare.

Question 1: What is the *purpose* of the gathering? Why are you bringing people together? What do you want to get out of the exercise, for your company, your organisation, your department or yourself?

Pinpoint the purpose and then you may achieve it. Otherwise, the gathering may ask: Why are we wasting our time? Alternatively: If they come with a different object, then you have increased their chance to achieve it.

Question 2: Knowing what you want, how do you get it? Do you make your purpose frankly known or do you approach your *target* more subtly, from the side? Discuss your strategy and your tactics with your trusted colleagues. Share your problem.

Conversely: If the meeting is designed to win over adversaries, then you must choose your conspirators with much greater care. The Board of a well-known company was so divided that its members were alleged to have started stabbing each other in the front! If your meeting turns into a battle-ground, face the front and guard your back.

Question 3: Who comes? Your *audience* may choose itself or you may be able to select. Either way, ask: Should the meeting be subdivided? Who should be included and who excluded? Who would help and who hinder? Whom can you call on for constructive suggestions, primed interventions or supportive comment? Whom should you either not invite or isolate, keep apart or set up as a target?

There are horses for courses, but always a limit on the number allowed in a race.

Question 4: What is the best *venue* for your purposes?

Subject to the limitations of comfort and perspiration, the more packed the audience, the livelier the atmosphere and the simpler the task of the speaker. Better to pack 30 into a room for 25 than 50 into one with seats for 100. Better to have standing room only than empty chairs. The experienced meeting organiser looks for an overflow. Next time, they will come early ... This time, it will be far easier to ignite the attention and to keep the interest of the audience.

Question 5: What *equipment* will you need?

If the room is a hall, check amplification. Where will you get it? How will it be operated and by whom? Who will fix it if it goes wrong? Will you need a standing or a table mike – and if so, will it be detachable and will the lead be long enough for those speakers who (like myself) wish to rove? Or should you have a neck mike? Or perhaps it would be worth paying for the flexibility of a radio mike?*

Whatever you choose, make sure that it is in position, ready and working, well before the starting time of the meeting. If the stand of the mike is to be adjustable, then check it. Nothing is more disconcerting to nervous speakers than 'stand rings' which in theory adjust but are in practice rusted into place, so that the user either has to crane the neck upwards or lean the face downwards.

---

*For microphones and techniques, see Chapter 42.

Which leads to questions 6 and 7: Will you need to prepare any, and if so what, *documentation**? And will you use any, and if so which, types of *visual aid**?

Prepared documentation saves time and heightens understanding. Will you require attenders to study, know and understand the material in advance – in which case, how far ahead will you supply it and to whom? Will they read or use it or simply file or lose it? Anyway, will they understand it without the explanation and exhortation which they will receive at the meeting? If supplied on the spot, will they use it to supplement the presentations or will it provide an unwanted distraction?

Or is it best to supply the documentation after the meeting, as a stimulant to both memory and action? Or will you then get complaints that it should have been available for study in advance or for use at the time?

Once you decide on the purpose of the documentation, you can then prepare it. Should you do so yourselves or pass it out to your graphics department or for outside experts? What impression do you wish it to give? What are you prepared to spend on its preparation?

Remember: Documentation is vital to the winning of court cases because it is more reliable than memory. As a witty Judge put it: 'As time goes on, memory fades – but recollection improves!' Documentation with presentations should be designed with care to provide precise, permanent and provably received information.

Documentation for meetings should be – but too often is not – professionally prepared, and pruned of all inessentials. While it should contain all that you would emphasise, it should omit any item that you would not wish to be held and proved against you.

Visual aids should be just that – aids through vision ... pointers and additions to speech, not substitues for it. In brief:

● Avoid, where possible, slides, which have to be shown in semi-darkness ... contained in a carousel, inflexible

*Details in Chapter 39.

and in pre-set order ... and to which the presenter can only point, if at all, with one of those awful, will-o'-the-wisp, tinkerbell-arrow torches. Slide shows are only suitable for post-prandial meetings, when you do not mind if the audience dozes off in the darkness – or where the gathering is counted by the hundred.

● Instead, use an overhead projector with transparencies. The best projectors are silent and mirrored – not fan-cooled relics of meetings which Noah held with his animals in the Ark. Transparencies themselves should be professional. But the expert should be warned that simplicity is best – black print on plain background ... and away with those awful, unfunny cartoon illustrations!

● Each transparency should be properly framed in cardboard and each frame marked with the subject and carefully laid out in advance of the meeting, on the table and alongside the (pre-prepared and focused) projector.

● Do not despise the old-fashioned flip board, newsprint and crayons. But ensure that the easel is firm, the pegs well in place – meetings disintegrate when props collapse.

Question 8: Have you planned your *layout*? What goes and who sits where and how? Will you need a raised platform, a speaker's table, a rostrum or a lectern? Have you considered lighting, heating and that most ignored of all necessities – the right of your audience to breathe? Far too many good meetings are ruined simply because the necessities, to say nothing of the comfort and the convenience, of speakers and audience are ignored in advance and impossible to arrange in arrear.

Finally, question 9: Have you chosen, prepared and trained your *speakers* for their job?

Like all other arts, that of organising, preparing and (especially) addressing and controlling a meeting must be learned.

Why do so many business executives understand the need to train (for instance) operatives to operate, drivers to drive, computer boffins to calculate and to press the right buttons – while expecting those who run meetings to acquire the skill without training?

The two key performers at a meeting are the chairperson and the speaker. Those of us who teach each and both of the basic skills of the craft have long since ceased to wonder at their almost universal amateurism.

So when preparing your meetings, do not take for granted your chairperson or your speaker. Train them. If you do either job yourself, remember that no one walks with more discomfort than the shoemaker who goes unshod. Like the hairless barber, prescribing remedies for baldness, meeting-mongers who run poorly prepared gatherings deserve the irritation and ill-esteem which they will have richly gleaned.

So prepare your plans and your participants, your venue and your visual aids, your colleagues and yourself. Meetings properly prepared seldom fail. The unprepared – in meetings as in most other aspects of the business and the social worlds – invite failure.

● How should you record your meetings or speeches? Will it be enough to keep minutes and if so, will it be enough for you and someone else to keep notes at the time? Or should all or part of the proceedings be put on tape? If so, who will produce, install, operate, adjust and fix the equipment?

Finally, meetings do not begin and end with the gavel. So when planning ask:

● Where will participants meet when they arrive? Have you an anteroom . . . adequate toilets . . . and telephones? Will your guests join the Board for a preliminary drink? Who will need refreshments and who will provide them and where and when?

● Will you allow smoking? If so, then should seats or rows or tables or areas be reserved for smokers – or for non-smokers? Smokers will need ashtrays. Will you also provide cigarettes, cigars, lighters?

● If the meeting is worth recording, participants will make notes. Why not provide them with ballpoints or pencils (the former are better – who has pencil sharpeners these days?)

● If the meeting is late or long, should you produce biscuits ... sandwiches ... a light meal? And how about (at least) clean, cool water, with glasses ... or hot coffee (in a vacuum flask?), with uncracked cups? Or maybe a glass of sherry, either before the meeting, to establish cordiality – or after it, to seal the day? Refreshment creates relaxation – and the knowledge that it is available is a marvellous shortener of meetings. Care for the comforts of those who attend and they will bless you – and return.

28 The Perils of Over-preparing

The well-planned meeting is one that recognises that not too much is likely to go as planned. A sensible chairperson will prepare both agenda and defences for trouble expected. The problem item then sails through without discussion and a seemingly innocuous, innocent and entirely uncontroversial matter flames into angry outburst. A meeting has the taunting unpredictability of a human being, multiplied by the number present.

So make due allowance for the certainty of error. Only the past is definite, and unless your minutes are sufficiently precise, even that is capable at best of mutual misunderstanding and at worst of revisionist re-interpretation.

So if you prepare or chair a meeting, you can only hope to sidestep trouble if you recognise its inevitability. Both in the preparation and in the presentation of a gathering, you must stay on your intellectual toes. As the only reliable prophets have been dead for at least two thousand years, you will achieve your best by preparing for the worst.

As with the meeting itself, so with the participants. The set speech is predestined to failure because it is prepared without knowing what others will say or have said or would wish to say.

Following the prepared vote of thanks in the league of

lingering nausea comes the set text, delivered either without regard to what has gone before or in deliberate repetition. 'It has been said many times this evening that..., but I must repeat that...' Or the speaker simply reads out the script without even bothering to note that it contains nothing but *déjà entendu*.

Ignoring the script, the speaker could have said: 'I congratulate Mr A for making the point that... He is of course right...' Or: 'I hope that we will all agree with Angela's theme that... It is a theme that I am pleased to emphasise. Perhaps I can put it into a slightly different context...'

Twist the tail of the language and it leaps into life. English is rich and vivid. Only the lazy tongue, the unread mind and the unwanted speaker will impoverish the meeting.

The parrot prepares by rote, but the most joyful parrot story concerns the only bird of its kind that rang the changes.

Ivan was a Moscow dissident who cheered himself up by teaching his parrot to repeat – in Russian, of course: 'To hell with the KGB!' One day, an agent of that august body knocked at Ivan's door. Quickly, he stuffed his parrot into the refrigerator.

The agent stepped in and without a word began to search the apartment. When he opened the door of the refrigerator, the parrot popped out. Ivan waited terrified, as the bird's beak opened. 'God bless the KGB!' it squawked, 'God bless the KGB!' Duly satisfied, the agent left the apartment.

Ivan took out his carving knife and sharpened it on a stone. 'Come over here', he said to the parrot. 'You little bastard! After only two minutes in Siberia, you already betray the cause!'

It is, of course, the human reader of the pre-prepared speech who should normally get the bird. The over-prepared speaker cannot react to the occasion or to the unexpected. Apart from the dangers of embalming words in type, you cannot control your audience if your eyes are on the paper. Eye contact is the first essential of successful speechmaking. That means – contacting the eyes of the audience and not concentrating your effort on your script.

The Times once defined riding as 'the art of keeping a horse between yourself and the ground'. To achieve that crucial result requires concentration, in the sure knowledge that, however well the steed is trained, the emergency is in the moment, in the movement, in the intervention of some outside force or factor. That, after all, is the challenge and the fun for the rider.

So it is with meetings. Prepare – the venue, the participants, the agenda, yourself. The challenge will come when there is nothing between your argument and its collapse other than your own quick wit and ingenuity, your ability to react to argument and to circumstance, your skill in controlling your own words and the reactions of others.

To over-prepare is as dangerous as to leave too much to chance. Whether you are in the chair or at the table, in charge or in the audience, you will be judged by your speed of reaction.

29 Seating the Meeting

Seating matters. So why do even businesspeople who willingly lavish cherished hours on seating their customers or clients so rarely spare a thought for seating meetings?

Fast-food operators carefully design plastic chairs which are comfortable enough for a swift swallow, but would scarcely entice a customer to outstay the briefest of productive welcomes. Airlines have long operated under Eddie Rickenbacker's call for maximum 'bums on seats', which involves designing the maximum number of tolerable seats jammed into the minimum area. Yet meeting-mongers are too prone to ram rears into whatever receptacles happen to be available. Thus, for instance:

● Participants are forced to sit for agonising hours in chairs without support for back or arms. Especially if you must have stackable seats, choose those that are contoured for comfort.

● With insufficient room around the table, late-comers collapse into armchairs or onto couches, out of view of the chair, so that their contribution to the proceedings may be measured in snores. Which is fine, if their sleep is your object.

Seating should be adequate and comfortable, allowing

mind and body alike to stretch. The longer the meeting, the greater the need for sensible comfort.

Then look at space. No sardine swam voluntarily into its can, so why should human beings with choice be stuffed together, elbow to rib, knee to groin?

If the meeting is small, then put participants around a table, with supportive chairs and ample spread for papers and documents.

For more participants, use more, smaller tables. The boardroom monster breeds distance and formality.

Wise communicators remove barriers between themselves and their listeners. The speaker moves around the table . . . executives invite guests to sit on chairs alongside . . . so break down the barriers at your larger meeting:

- Place your tables in herringbone formation, leaving a corridor down the centre. Avoid the serried regimentation of parallel lines.

- If there is no room for tables, try theatre-style seating, with a writing attachment for each.

- Cinema or lecture room style, with immobile banked seating, may suit you. I dislike it deeply because the room is as immobile and inflexible as the participants. The classroom is for the student, not for the mature meeting.

The room should be large enough to hold the meeting in comfort, but small enough to retain and maintain atmospheric intimacy. If the furniture is movable, the illusion of a compact audience may be combined with the reality of sufficient space.

If your meeting is a conference . . . a large seminar . . . then apply the same basic rules. Empty spaces create poor communications, but overcrowding induces potential listeners to leave those spaces even emptier. The organiser of the meeting, large or small, gives crafty thought to these problems while choice is available.

30 Plant Culture

'May I congratulate the Rt. Hon. lady on her success in...' proclaims the loyalist at Prime Minister's Question Time. Opposition shouts of: 'Give him a job!' Unperturbed, the questioner continues: 'And can the Prime Minister now tell us what are her proposals concerning the future of that operation?'

The Prime Minister picks up her looseleaf file, with its prepared and potted answers, and reads out an exemplary reply. Opposition shouts of: 'Plant!'

Irrespective of the political colour of the Government, this method of ensuring that you get asked the questions which you wish to answer is normal procedure, disliked by those who resent the pre-emption of their twice-weekly fifteen minutes of savagery, but designed to turn attention to those aspects of government policy which are regarded as at least apparently worthy of praise.

As in so many respects, it is worth studying and copying Parliamentary procedures if you wish to command a meeting. Plant culture is an art worth studying.

You are promoting a new project? Then consider: Would it be more acceptable if the ideas emerged from you? Or, more likely, should you not father it off on a respected colleague – perhaps someone whose paternity would surprise the meeting?

You wish to open an operation in (say) Birmingham or Leicester? Then get a colleague from Glasgow or Gillingham to propose that the Midlands would provide easiest access by road and rail. You need to close down a plant in the North? Then look to that area for someone to say: 'Unfortunately, we cannot continue . . .'

I once joined with British colleagues in promoting a Commonwealth organisation. We hoped that the HQ would be in London, where we could direct operations (we thought) most successfully. I quietly suggested to a Canadian colleague the possibility of putting the HQ in Ottawa. As I hoped, he retorted: 'No good. The Secretariat is in London. That is the centre of Commonwealth activity and everyone has to pass through your capital. Anyway, it will be useful for us to have you at the centre, as a UK Parliamentarian.'

So the idea was self-sown. He told the meeting: 'I would like to thank our UK colleagues for kindly agreeing that the HQ of our new organisation should be in London. We know that this will impose heavy burdens on them, but they will be doing great service to us all.'

Our Canadian colleague had asked me to propose London from the chair and I had declined. 'If you suggest it and the meeting wants it, then I agree . . . but the initiative must come from you . . .' No problem.

To take root, your plant must be placed in fertile soil. Think carefully before you decide what result to seek. I will not forget the colleague who addressed a meeting thus: 'I myself would have preferred to do such-and-such. But I have been asked by Mr Janner to propose that . . . and to say that the idea was mine . . .!'

Do you not wonder sometimes how people who are so dim and whose fathers are insufficiently placed to exercise nepotism can get so far, whether in commerce or in politics? The grafting of ideas should always be onto well-tried stock.

Finally: What of the planting of blame? You miss an appointment? It is your fault, but you cannot admit it? Then your secretary may have to telephone and say: 'I am so sorry. I forgot to remind him.' The person taking the blame may have to make the primary and private atonement. In public, though, you must accept the responsibility.

The best leaders have the trust and confidence of their followers or subordinates because they accept public responsibility. The British Civil Service thrives because Ministers take the blame for the mistakes of their Departments and are not permitted by custom, etiquette and good decency to proclaim: 'My advisors got it wrong.' If you are out in front, then by all means plant ideas, questions or suggestions. They should bear better fruit than if they appeared to come from you. To assign blame is poor management – of men and of meetings alike.

31 Checklist for the Chair

If you are taking the chair at any meeting, prepare for battle. As the angler reviews his tackle, so you must assess your arrangements and the needs of the meeting or you are inviting the failure which you will deserve. Here is your list of the most important items to be checked before the meeting starts.

● Have you chosen the best venue for your purpose? Will it hold comfortably and cosily the numbers expected? If not, can you move? If in doubt as to numbers, how can you achieve flexibility – within the room or hall or by switching to another when the time comes?

● What is the best layout for the venue? Will you need (eg) a platform or dais? How should the seats be set up so as to fill the space, to provide comfort and access, and to allow for the needs of the participants – and what are they?

● Will you require other facilities in the room – tables, desks, ashtrays etc. – and who will provide them, how and when?

● What other facilities will be required and will they be available – from toilets to telephones, from refreshments to meals and accommodation?

- Will special arrangements be needed for delegates or speakers, to ensure their safe arrival, their comfort and convenience, their prompt and satisfactory departure?

- What other equipment will be needed for the conduct of the meeting itself? Check in particular: microphones; visual aids; lectern.

- Who will look after the logistics – from water for speakers to arrangements with caterers? Who will be at your side, to guide you on procedures or people or to sort out the problems which will inevitably arise? Whom else will you need and for what – from passing microphones to questioners to checking in arrivals and providing them with documentation? Who will arrange and supervise the staffing?

- Who will speak and in what order? Have you prepared the programme – formal or informal? If you expect guest speakers, who will check on whether they have got the right date, place and time, so as to maximise their chances of prompt and contented arrival? Who will welcome them and how and where? Are you sufficiently briefed to introduce them – or have you arranged for the introduction and briefing by others?

- Do you know the rules of procedures, the regulations or standing orders, which will govern the conduct of the meeting? If not, then to whom can you turn if you run into trouble?

- How will you seat your committee, your colleagues, your guests? Who will you need at your side, to provide you with guidance or convey your messages to others? How should you arrange seating and placing, so as to cater for the sensitivities and *amour propre* of key or prickly participants?

- Have you assigned all necessary roles? Are they known at least to those who will take them? For instance: Who will introduce or thank; propose, second, oppose or seek the rejection of motions or resolutions? Who could or should you tip off to do what and when and how?

● Have you consulted with colleagues – lay or professional – about the best ways to win – or the least conspicuous ways to lose? Have you prepared your troops for battle?

● Are you yourself prepared? Have you your documentation and your notes, your agenda well annotated, your file in order? Are you adequately fed, emptied, relaxed, calm and confident? If not, then how can you achieve these – the basic necessities – before the meeting starts?

Arrive on time and ready and your meeting is half won. Turn up late and unprepared and you deserve to lose.

PART IV

MEETINGS –
SPECIAL
AND
VARIOUS

Introduction to Part IV

So far, we have looked at general rules. This Part considers some of the special meetings which you may have to chair, to address, to convince or to satisfy. These include company gatherings, conferences, seminars and those most crucial of all meetings: close-up and over meals.

32 Committees

A committee is a gathering or group to which subjects or problems are 'committed'. As the dead are committed to their graves, so unwanted aspirations and sometimes people are buried in committee.

However: Worthwhile committees create and (especially) evolve ideas. These are normally then returned to the main body as recommendations – for implementation or (sometimes) for destruction.

In general, the smaller the committee, the better its results. I work closely with a spirited, retired businessman who works (as he puts it) on the basis that every committee should be made up of an odd number of people, and three is too many! In practice, even he cloaks his virility with a decent garb of apparent democracy.

In Parliament, committees range in size from small, party or all-party groups, for the promotion of a rainbow variety of objectives, to a 'Committee of the Whole House' which deals with Finance Bills and other matters of constitutional impact.

If you are forming a committee, you should:

● Decide with precision the purposes of the committee and then work out its proposed terms of reference.

- In the light of those purposes and terms, select members most likely to achieve your results.

- Feed in not only your appropriate colleagues, but where necessary, people from outside – remembering to seek involvement and enthusiasm from those who have the complete range of experience and knowledge required.

- Within the limits of the above, keep the committee as small as possible.

Before the first meeting, prepare your ground. Brief your allies. Decide who will be best in the chair . . . as secretary . . . as treasurer . . . Then ensure that those people (who may or may not include yourself) will be duly proposed, seconded and supported.

Then to work. At the first meeting, you discuss your terms of reference and how the committee will operate, by whom it will be led and staffed. You present an agenda, prepare for minutes, discuss additions and, where necessary, seek guidance.

As for the conduct of the committee meetings, the rules are essentially no different from any others. They will depend upon its structure, membership, traditions, standing orders or normal way of doing business. The chairperson chairs the meeting with firmness and fairness; sees that it gets through its business with despatch and involvement; and is responsible for any report back.

It is sometimes asserted that if Moses had been a committee, the Children of Israel would still be in Egypt. He was not. But in the modern world of business and every other sort of organisation, committees are essential components. Moses would have had to learn how to get his own way by following the path of careful committee conduct, or his flock would have spent even more than 40 years in the desert. Indeed, had he done so, it is possible that he might have turned in another direction and ended up in some other part of the Middle East, with sensible oil resources!

33 General Meetings

In broad terms, meetings may be divided into two categories – 'general' and 'special'. A 'general' meeting is one that deals with a broad spectrum of subjects, while a 'special' is aimed at one or more specific subjects.

For instance: each year, each company will have its Annual General Meeting – its AGM. So will most societies or organisations. The officers will report; the year will be reviewed; the accounts will be presented and (usually) approved; required elections will be held; and shareholders will have their annual opportunity to question those responsible.

A special meeting may be convened in accordance with the rules or *ad hoc*. For instance: If the rules themselves are to be altered, this may have to be done at a special meeting, although this may itself be part of a general meeting. In order not to have to convene a meeting specially for the purpose, notice may be given that at a specified time the normal or general meeting will be adjourned and a special meeting held, for the purpose stated.

Whether the meeting is general or special, appropriate notice will have to be given. This in itself may depend what resolutions are to be presented. The rules of any company and of most organisations will provide for appropriate notice in respect of specified types of resolution. In the case of a company, check the Articles of Association, which will probably be based on Table A of the Companies Act 1948. In the case of a society or organisation, check its constitution.

Both general and special meetings should follow and complete their agendas, and then adjourn.

34 The Annual General Meeting

Not surprisingly, most Annual General Meetings are held once a year! All should be. Companies are required by law to do this and most other organisations by their rules or traditions. Anyway, once in each year, the body should check on its health.

In practice, the AGM itself may be less important than the discipline of preparing for it, which must include:

- *Chairman's Report* – to contain the distilled essentials of the year's business or operations, generally flavoured by opinion.

- *Accounts* for the appropriate period, accompanied by the treasurer's report, also complete with opinion and generally replete with exhortations.

- *Resolutions* – ordinary, special and extraordinary – of which (where necessary and according to the rules) appropriate notice will have been given.

With an eye to time, place and business, you draw up the agenda and then survey it for likely trouble. You may spot it without difficulty and then prepare your troops, your allies and your speakers. Instinct sharpened by experience may indicate pleasant pastures which conceal minefields, in which case, you may want to sweep them in advance, with quiet words to the right people.

You may be assured, though, that in any well-organised AGM of any interest anything that can go wrong probably will. Those items for which you have prepared will slide through with a smile. The trouble lurks in some unexpected corner.

Preparations for, proceedings at and records of an AGM should be made by experts – Company Secretaries, accountants or lawyers. Requirements are set out in Articles of Association; in a Statutory Instrument replacing Table A of the Companies Act, 1985; and in a series of provisions in the Act itself. These include such matters as the quorum; chairman; voting, including polls and proxies; resolutions – ordinary, extraordinary and special; adjournments; minutes and minute books. Company meetings should be conducted in accordance with guidance and rules in this book but always with the aid of those expert in the law and in its specific application.

To summarise: there are three broad types of meetings of members of the company: AGM; Extraordinary General Meeting; and separate meetings of classes of shareholders. As we have seen, AGM legislation is compulsory. Under Sections 366 and 367 of the 1985 Act, an AGM must be held at least once each calendar year and not later than 15 months after the last meeting. Extraordinary General Meetings (EGMs) must also comply with Section 368 of the Act. Members have the right to requisition an EGM where over 10 percent of the voting membership (in value) requires such a meeting.

In most other respects, though, the legislation on the regulation of company meetings is simply an alternative to whatever the companies decide to include in their Articles. The 'model rules' are contained in the old Table A of the 1948 Companies Act, but in the recent consolidation these have now been issued as a Statutory Instrument (805/1985).

35 Conferences and Seminars

The word 'conference' covers a multitude of modern meetings. In theory and by definition, it is a gathering for people to confer. In practice, it may be a (perhaps) more acceptable description of a seminar – a meeting at which people are more likely to learn from a lecturer, presenter or guru than from each other. Names do matter, so select the one most acceptable for your event – and then plan for success.

First, the venue: Check:

- Position: Accessibility and convenience for the maximum number of attenders – including (where appropriate) availability of road, rail or air services; vulnerability of attenders to unnecessary interruptions. It is often worth hiring outside premises for company conferences.

- Facilities – meals and refreshments; car parking; clean and adequate toilets – plus (if appropriate) swimming, golf or other recreation.

- Rooms – for meeting or (if required) sleeping; and, if flexibility may be required (in case you cannot estimate numbers with precision) or variety (for syndicates, perhaps), then is it available in accommodation and in pricing?

- Cost – as compared to other venues; including nature and extent of cancellation fees; extras etc.

- Adequacy, courtesy, efficiency and kindness of staffing – and availability of both staff and premises in good time to prepare – including setting out of tables, chairs etc. and (especially) preparation of amplification and lighting, setting out of documentation etc.

Next: Preparation of programme and speakers. Check:

- What do you wish to achieve and how can it best be done – with maximum cost effect and minimum time and trouble?

- Which and how many speakers or presenters will be needed – and what would they charge?

- Will you need any and if so what visual aids – from film and video to overhead projector and flip charts?

- What documentation should be provided – and when – ie for delegates to study beforehand (but who will do so – and who will forget to bring it with them?) and/or at the time and/or as follow up – and who will draft and prepare it?

If you are marketing a conference for which attenders are expected to pay – whether on an organisational break-even or on a profit basis, then:

- What should you charge? What will people be prepared to pay and with what expectations?

- How do you gather in your delegates? What marketing material will you need, what will it cost, who will prepare and print it and how will you put it before the eyes of your most likely punters, at minimum – and at what – cost and with maximum effect?

Whatever the nature or type of your conference, you must inevitably decide:

- Who should be in overall charge, holding the reins and making necessary decisions?

- To whom will the organiser be responsible; how much independence will he or she be given; what reporting arrangements will be needed; and how will the best communication be achieved with the least misunderstanding?

So you make, prepare and firm up your plans and then the event arrives:

- What type of and how many staff will be needed and where will you find them?

- Who will chair the meeting; what part will the Chair take and has he or she been properly briefed (not least about the speakers, including introductory material, their timing and their roles).

- How will attenders be greeted on arrival and by whom – and will they need documentation, badges, refreshments etc. and if so, then who will provide them and how and where?

- Who will look after: Meals, accommodation, VIPs and visitors – and cater for special needs or complaints?

- Is the seating satisfactory – or does it need shifting, perhaps in a coffee break; can everyone see without neck craning or discomfort; and are smokers separated from non-smokers – and with adequate ashtrays?

- Have you checked ventilation, amplification, heating, lighting – and are all operating as desired – and if not, then how can the deficiencies be met and by whom – and how swiftly?

- Preparing for the follow-up, have you given delegates assessment or appraisal sheets – and when and by whom should these be collected?

- Apart from leaving delegates with whatever message you need to implant, what other goods, products or documents should be displayed or otherwise put into delegates' hands?

If the conference is held in conjunction with an exhibition, then you need an expert – your own or hired – to plan, prepare, set up, supervise and dismantle the exhibits . . . collect, brief and otherwise prepare the exhibitors . . . and co-ordinate the entire operation.

When the conference is over, that leaves the follow-up:

● Have the desired results been obtained and how do you know? Who collects the assessment sheets and makes the appropriate appraisal?

● Will you need a follow-up conference – of organisers, participants or any (and if so, which) others – and when and who will prepare, address and brief it?

● Taking all the successes and failures, triumphs and errors into account, will you want a repeat – and if so, on what basis, where, when and how – and especially: how will you avoid making the same mistakes again?

With conferences and seminars, as with all other meetings and gatherings, you get out what you put in. The greater the effort in preparation and presentation . . . the more the resources in hours, people and money that you are prepared to put in, the better the results you should get.

36 Conventions

The greater the gathering, the weightier the potential problems. Foremost among them: Conference committees.

If you are organising a large-scale conference (hereinafter, for convenience, referred to as 'a convention'), you will have to prepare for it. That job should be handed over to a *programme committee*. Its chairperson should be experienced and hardworking, acceptable and wise. Its members should be knowledgeable and malleable, and cover the full range of those attending.

A convention seeks a consensus. The programme committee is its microcosm.

So include the young and the old, the left and the right, the traditional and the radical, in whatever sphere you cover. Propose them to your executive or other governing body. Better still: Plant the proposals among those attending or get a respected but absent citizen to write a letter saying: 'I am so sorry that I cannot be with you because of . . . but I would respectfully suggest the setting up of a programme committee, which might well include such redoubtable colleagues as . . .'

Flatter the 'colleagues' and they are unlikely to turn down the invitation. Call them together not too often, but always with a plan or a paper to discuss, paragraph by paragraph, point by point.

It is the programme committee that should plot the course of the convention, day by day, hour by hour. How many speakers do you need and on what subjects? Who is bright in both reputation and speech? Who will draw the audience and prod their minds? Mix old stars with young talent. Your programme should have as much variety as commercial vaudeville. If you wish your delegates to be pleased, then instruct your programme committee to choose speakers who will not bore.

Well directed, the programme committee will ensure that there are enough guests to provide novelty, but sufficient time for the delegates to hear their favourite sound, that of their own voices. They may have travelled far for that joy. They may dine for ever off the tale of how they held the floor at your convention. Then ensure that your programme committee gives them their minutes – but not other people's hours.

The programme committee should also decide on the breakdown of meetings – into committees, subcommittees or (to use the current terms) 'workshops' or 'syndicates'. The more numerous the groups, the greater the number of speakers; the more the speakers, the greater the satisfaction.

Once the sessions are worked out, the programme committee will propose on whom the spotlight shall fall. In particular: who will chair and who act as rapporteur, bringing back the message of the minor group to the mass of the plenary?

With skill and judgement, the speakers will fill the bill, but not too much. It is a much greater disaster to have so many guests that you have no time for the conferees to confer than too few. If you run out of guests, if your convention has any substance, you can usually find someone substantial to fill the gap with distinction.

Next: Select your *steering committee*. If you wish, your pre-convention programme committee can have new life as the steering committee, which (as its respected name implies) will steer the gathering through its daily problems, arguments, disputes and procedural aggravations.

People who are good at planning in private and in peace may be poor in power or under pressure or in public. Or you may simply want to give extra glories to important people who need to be on committees to satisfy either their own vanity or pride or that of those whom they represent and who will be upset if their name does not appear on the printed programme. So you may perfer to have different faces on your steering committee.

Then you may need a *nominations committee*. This small but eminent body of leaders, selected from the top drawer, will decide who to nominate for the various offices. In a controlled democracy, their nominees will probably get the jobs. In others, they will decide on and prepare the list of candidates. Or if nominations are received in advance, they will sort them out and, together with the steering committee, set up the appropriate election procedures.

Finally: Your convention may make resolutions. It may wish to summarise its view on key issues, either for its own benefit or (more likely) to put out to the press or public. In that case, create a *resolutions committee*. Its members should include people who are politically intelligent and experienced and linguistically articulate. A lawyer or two will do you no harm; plus a senior offical of the organisation; and one or two people from your executive body. While all three other committees *should* be kept small, the larger the resolutions committee *must* be, the greater the task and the more likely the bungle.

When the resolutions committee has either decided or been instructed as to the nature of the resolutions required, it should depute one or two of its members to knock out the first draft. This is then brought to the committee, which knocks it into a shape fit to go before the convention.

By creating and using these four committees, you ensure adequate preparation by skilled people; proper discussion in advance and at the time; a greater prospect of success for the work of the convention; and a greater spread for the blame in case of catastrophe. The larger the convention, the more sensible the custom of organising it through the committee system.

37 Close-up Magic

Magicians generally specialise in one of two types of presentation – stage work or 'close-up'. Some techniques are similar
for both; others are not. As with the magic of sleight of
hand, misdirection and illusion, so with that of words. Either
way, you must look your audience in the eye, but when
the meeting is eyeball to eyeball, error is easier to observe
and much harder to cover up.

Queen Victoria once complained of her Prime Minister,
William Gladstone: 'He speaks to Me as if I were a public
meeting!' Even his wife shared the sovereign's irritation. 'If
you weren't such a great man,' she told him, 'you'd be a
terrible bore!'

Gladstone's great rival, Benjamin Disraeli, enchanted his
Queen. 'I grew intoxicated with my own eloquence,' he once
said. But he directed that eloquence at his audience. Remembering (to quote from one of his fictional characters) that
everyone's idea of an agreeable person is someone who agrees
with him, he would tell his sovereign what she wanted to
hear. 'Everyone likes flattery,' he told Matthew Arnold. 'And
when you come to Royalty you should lay it on with a trowel!'
He did. On one occasion, he even told the Queen: 'Your
Majesty is the head of the literary profession!' She believed
him.

When you deal with individuals, do not treat them as a public meeting. Recognise them, their likes and their hates. Flatter them, their esteem and their views. Hope that they will accept you and your ideas – but be determined that even if they reject your message, they will at least respect the messenger.

Even with the largest of meetings, every listener should feel that the speaker's words are aimed at him or her. You must make eye contact. Still: From afar, glazed or wandering eyes may go unobserved. In close-up, never. The death of a deal or of a friendship is sealed by those familiar words: 'He kept looking over my shoulder . . .' Or 'There's something shifty about her. She wouldn't look me in the eye.'

An 'iris' has been defined as 'the part of the eye that smiles – as in the song: "When Iris Eyes are Smiling"!' Smile with your mouth only and a large audience may miss your insincerity. From nearby, the audience will take due note.

So look into the iris of your close-up audience, and listen. You can learn a little while you are talking and much when silent. To be acclaimed as a good conversationalist, try letting others do the talking. Talk is always cheap because supply feeds demand.

Look your companion or adversary in the eye; listen; then put your case in a tone and volume suited to the private meeting, not the public gathering.

If a bore is someone who interrupts *you*, do not yourself interrupt your listener's word flow. But do be prepared to concede to others the right to stop and question you. In close-up, courtesy is crucial. At a public meeting, either you or the Chair or both may ignore or curtail or demand silence from the interrupter. From close-up, you need subtlety to turn the conversation in your direction.

Address a public meeting and you talk *at* your audience. Privately, you converse *with* them. A formal speech passes in one direction; a conversation is two-way traffic in ideas. To sell yours, you must at least consider other people's.

When setting up your private meeting, then, choose time, place and occasion with an eye to the convenience of your companion or quarry. Then ensure that there is a meeting of minds. Woo your audience and, even without the magic of Disraeli, you will win. Address it as a public meeting and, even with the intellect of Gladstone, you will lose both your listener and your case.

The more private or informal the meeting, the more careful you should be about taking notes.* But if anything said may be (literally as well as metaphorically) on the record, then the note-taking should be known to all.

Suppose that you meet a Minister on official business. You will either sit informally in armchairs or, more likely, around a table, either in the Minister's office or in an interview room. A civil servant will be in attendance, pen and pad at the ready. In those circumstances, where the host is to have notes, I have always reckoned that the same advantage should be mine. If the Minister is accompanied, so am I. If his aide takes a record, so does mine.

This arrangement can go wrong. I once led a delegation to see Prime Minister Thatcher at No. 10. She received us in the upstairs drawing room, with gracious courtesy. Her aides were present.

The Secretary-General of my organisation quietly took a note at the back. 'I thought this was a private and informal meeting,' said the Prime Minister, looking at the offending note-taker. The moment was uncomfortable and the meeting never fully recovered.

So: if in doubt, ask. 'I see that your assistant is taking a note. Do you have any objection to our doing the same?' Or: 'Perhaps it would be better if we treated this meeting as totally off the record? Certainly I would not want this part of the conversation to be recorded...' The aide will be told to put away his pen. Of course, you should recognise that in due course a memo will be made from memory.

Travelling abroad, I often visit leaders of other lands, sometimes in the company of the British Ambassador or High Commissioner. I cannot ever remember anyone taking a note. But it is part of a diplomat's job to record essentials and to pass them back to HQ.

I have learned to do the same. As soon as possible after

---

*See Chapter 40, for the techniques of note using.

a crucial meeting, I dictate my recollection into a machine, where possible in company with someone who was present with me. In the hours or days that follow, I remember other chunks of the conversation and add riders. The notes are often cryptic – meaningless to anyone other than myself, so as never to risk betraying a confidence, while not forgetting to take properly into account what others wish me to know and remember – or they would not have told me.

38 Mealtime Meetings

Meetings, like Napoleon's armies, march on their stomachs. If the repast – food, drink, company and speeches – are satisfactory, then the battle is well won. Fail in any aspect and the feast and your good relations will be equally poisoned.

Your planning starts with purpose and with numbers. What do you wish to achieve and who should be there? What atmosphere do you seek and how can you best achieve it?

Then: What is the best venue? Will you sit round one table or many? Who will sit where and by whom?

With the hindsight of too many mistakes, here are some of our hints on the planning of feeding:

- Compatibility of company is far more important at meals than at any other time because there is no escape. Select with care – and if in doubt separate potential incompatibles.

- Avoid if possible a top table. Try putting the guest speaker at a table in the centre and seating distinguished colleagues at different ends of the table or at different tables spread through the room.

- Try to fill your room. Cabaret is the most difficult of all the arts of entertainment. Speakers must be seen as well as heard and should not be talking to or across wide open spaces.

- Even a last-minute check of your seating plan and guest list will produce errors and omissions. Check it.

- Brief your chairperson as to time and speakers, as well as purpose and priorities.

- Brief speakers. Tell them in advance to whom they will be speaking; about what; for how long; and with what purpose.

- Check acoustics and (if necessary) amplification equipment and visual aids.

- Consider documentation – including organisational information, briefing or promotional material.

Next: How will you shape your meal meeting? Place yourself or key colleagues between those whom you wish to influence. Allow time for business talk between courses. The smaller the gathering though, the better you can arrange a 'working' occasion, listening to the guest or presenter between courses or (better still) mouthfuls. For relaxation, words and wine mix well.

If the occasion is one for protocol, then how can you best get it out of the way? The 'Loyal Toast' precedes smoking and should come before the coffee. If the session is to be lengthy, a watering break is thoughtful and improves concentration.

Do not let your occasion overrun. Breakfast meetings are an American aberration which we are acquiring. They must finish on time or people will wander away. Meetings over lunch are equally dangerous, especially if people need to leave, but do not like to do so for fear of causing offence. Even the dinner gathering may evaporate in less than good spirits.

Boredom, then, is the ultimate enemy of mealtime meetings. So resist the temptation to put in more speakers, for the salvation of pride and so that offence may not be caused to a few who want 'just a few words', at the expense of the many who will have heard too many.

PART V

VISUAL AIDS, ACCESSORIES – AND KINDRED ARTS

39 Visual Aids

In the days before visual aids, a speaker's only instruments were voice and personality. Today, a variety of aids can brighten any meeting, adding lucidity, colour and edge to any message. Used without preparation, understanding, skill and care, they may also do harm, detracting attention from the speaker's words, deflecting interest from content to techniques and irritating the listeners.

So here is your guide, as promoter, speaker or in the chair, to visual aids, their use and their abuse.

General rules

By definition, visual aids are intended to help speaker and speech, not to replace them. So resist the temptation to gather your audience, draw the curtains, lower the screen, switch on the video or film and then relax.

Instead: Consider the purpose of the gathering . . . what you wish to put across . . . and how best to do it. Who should speak and explain? Then: What backing does that person need, so as to add bite, clarity and interest to the presentation? What information is better conveyed by sight, rather than or in addition to sound?

Documentation

If words are better read than spoken, write them. If the message of a presentation can be condensed on paper, so as to make it easier to follow at the time or to check thereafter, prepare the papers.

The more crucial the occasion, the more careful and professional you must be. A batch of photocopied sheets clipped, stapled or strung together may do for an informal meeting with colleagues. To confront clients or customers, actual or prospective . . . to present a proposal, a quote or an estimate – that requires documentation well printed, properly numbered and indexed and encased in a neat file or folder.

Do you provide the documentation in advance? As already discussed in Chapter 27: yes – if the recipients are likely to read it, unlikely to lose it or to forget to bring it with them to the meeting; and if the documents need to be assimilated in advance, while not needing explanation to be understood. Otherwise – no. Provide them at the time and explain why they were not supplied beforehand.

When I address meetings – conferences, seminars or any other – I restrict documentation to the minimum and usually provide only:

● Copies of charts, transparencies and other visual aids – so as to save my listeners the trouble of copying them as we go along – a process which would distract them from their listening; and

● Supplementary pamphlets, handouts, marketing material or other documents which may be useful to the audience but which are not essential to the presentation.

Boards

Black or white . . . with chalk or wipeable colour or magnetic attachments. One form of board or another has assisted instructors since the days of the Pharaohs and beyond. Advantages: minimal cost, ready availability and easy use. Disadvantages: Inelegance and the need to wipe out before rewriting.

Flip charts and newsprint

I prefer the almost equally ancient flip chart – simple, easy to operate and swiftly disposable. You can inscribe key words and ideas and concepts at will and whim and without fuss. You can also prepare sheets in advance. Once explained, they can be retained by flipping over or torn off and dumped, gently or with a flourish.

Remember: while writing, try not to turn your back on your audience. Write from the side. Use brief words and abbreviations. Omit vowels. Keep words and diagrams simple, and large enough to be read from the rear. Ensure that:

● the chart is well placed, so that it can be seen from any seat in the room; and

● it is firmly footed and screwed or plugged into place so that it will not collapse on use or touch. Boards placed on antique easels or inadequate, ill-fitting plugs invariably do collapse at the most visible and catastrophic moment. Diversions should be planned . . .

● writing materials are fresh, varied and adequate; marker pens are thick, of many colours, and have not dried up.

Transparencies and slides

The simpler the aid, the greater its effect and the less likely it is to go wrong in use. For any lengthy or detailed presentation, and for any audience of up to 300 or so people, I use 'transparencies' – charts, foils, call them what you will . . . overhead images, cast upwards by projector. For a vast meeting, you may need 35-millimetre slides on a carousel. Otherwise, the supreme advantages of 'overheads' are as follows:

- They provide flexibility. You move from one to another, changing their order if and at any time you wish ... move forward or backwards, at will or at whim – or in response to questions or to audience reaction. The change of carousel slide is not immediate – the pause-and-whirr syndrome is irritating and distracting.

- Overheads can almost always be controlled and best organised and operated by the speaker. You may need an assistant to deal with the mechanics of slide present-ation. Apart from the extra manpower, the assistant may miss cues and is even more likely to insert slides back-wards or upside down than you are – which means that:

- Slides on a carousel get mixed up, an irritating menace.

- Overhead transparencies may be altered up to the last minute. On many machines, you may (if you must, which should not be too often) use a revolving roll of plastic to make your own images as you go along. Slides take longer and are less easy to make, copy or duplicate.

- With transparencies, you may use special effects. Some presenters like the 'overlay', preparing and placing one image on the other. I dislike them and prefer separate and simple transparencies for each stage and build-up of the process.

Equipment

The best machinery is silent. Noisy, fan-cooled equipment is irritating, distracting and – because it will not necessarily switch off when you put out its light, it multiplies alterations in atmosphere. It is bulky, ugly and unloveable.

We choose and use simple, silent projectors, with the image shot onto the screen by mirror. Treat the mirror, though, with special care, in both use and storage. It scratches too easily. Also: Do not bang the table or the bulb will burst. Replacements are costly and presentations are interrupted by a blown bulb with the same twang and effect as a snapped string on a guitar or violin.

We bring our own mirror-projector to meetings and presentations and ensure that a spare (of every sort) is available in case of breakdown. Fuses, bulbs and machinery are even more vulnerable to breakdown than those who operate them.

Preparing transparencies

Your transparencies should be worthy of you and of your audience – professionally produced. But beware of the artistic graphics department or independent specialist, overfilling space with words or diagrams ... using dark backgrounds or infantile 'funnies' ...

The essentials of a first-class transparency are:

- Simplicity – few words, carefully chosen ... forceful, minimal graphs or charts, emphasising the essentials and omitting frills – or leaving them for separate viewing ... impact through brevity ...

- Visibility of content – black words, figures or lines on plain backgrounds are best, with colour for underlining or emphasis ...

- Wit and humour, used with discretion ... If you need artistry, employ an artist. Economy of line and word is worth paying for ...

Each transparency should be separately framed in firm card. Cards should be numbered in series, but put a brief, clear title at the top of each so that they can be spread out alongside the projector, like a bridge hand in the palm of the professional, with titles showing. In that way, you can see at a glance and immediately extract any one you need – no fuss, no scrabbling, no riffling through the pile ...

The screen

Set up your screen – preferably one that can be angled forward, so that you avoid 'keystoning', and leave your image neatly squared.

Then, with your projector tested and operative, your transparencies ordered and arranged . . . with a chair or stool available in case you need it, plus a lectern, if you want one . . . with your audience and yourself in each other's view – you are ready to begin.

Overhead presentation

The golden rules on the use of transparencies are these:

- Start with the first already in position. Switch on when needed.

- To change transparencies, use both hands. At the same moment as you remove the existing foil with your left hand, replace it with one in your right. The screen should never – then or at any other time – show a blank light.

- Point by placing a pen or pencil (not one that is round and rolling) onto the transparency . . . or by pointing with the shadow of your finger, or with a pointer, at the screen . . . or by covering part of the wording with paper or cardboard. The third method is infinitely the worst, because the audience concentrates on wondering what is hidden . . . and anyway, the cover may (and often does) fall off.

- When you do not want your audience to look at the screen, switch off the projector.

- Never let your unintended shadow obstruct any part of the screen. If you have to pass between projector and screen, perhaps to reach transparency or flip chart, switch off.

Slides

Like transparencies, slides should be professionally prepared ... basic and simple ... and with economy of line and content. Choose projector and carousel with care. The only alternative to a break between slides is to use twin machines, which is not generally satisfactory.

As you cannot alter the order of the slides or nip back and forth through the series, take particular care to plan the order in advance. Recognise that you will be stuck with it.

With the room in darkness, you could try spotlighting yourself. Point, if you must, with arrowed light or with the dim image of a billiard cue type of stick. Use the slide series and then switch on all the lights and talk to your audience.

Audio-visual

Video programmes, like cine films, may move a meeting, but they are the lazy presenter's way of bringing expertise to the audience. The risk of their taking over the occasion is even greater than with slides.

Because viewing – video or slides, like television – is non-demanding and non-participatory, it is rarely the best way to transfer ideas and to convey them into argument or action. By all means switch on the machinery immediately after a good meal, so that your audience can doze if they wish, unseen and uninterrupted. Or if you must address so many meetings for your company or organisation in so many places that you cannot cope without a video presentation from you, as a prologue or epilogue to a visual effort by a colleague or subordinate, so be it.

Remember, though, that the making of videos and films is time-consuming and costly and that a combination of economy and first-class results is hard to achieve because in this sphere, like most others, the principle of paying peanuts and getting monkeys usually applies ...

Presentational training

There is no substitute for personal presentation, but the pre-

senter must be trained. The video camera with skilled opera-
tor combined with a TV screen and microphone facilities
in working order, in the hands of expert trainers provide
incomparably the best method of training either presenters
or trainers.

Watch yourself at work and using other visual aids . . .
criticised by trainer and (perhaps) colleagues and (certainly)
by yourself . . . and you will learn more in two days with
visual aids than you could be taught in two weeks without
them.

40 Notes

Whether you are speaker or in the chair, you will need notes. Which raises the crucial questions: What notes are best for which occasion; who prepares them; and how do you best use and hold them?

The essential notes for the Chair are:

- The agenda – the order of proceedings (see Chapter 13).

- Notes for the Chair – item by (especially, contentious) item, prepared by the Secretary or other expert, if necessary in conjunction with the person who will chair the meeting – that preparation being of itself a useful discipline, forcing attention to likely problems.

- Names and details of any speakers.

- Notes of opening address, introduction to item or other contribution from the Chair.

- Special notes on specific items.

If the meeting is of size and substance, the Secretary (of the company, organisation etc.) should sit beside the Chair, checking the agenda and feeding through notes on items and speakers as they are required, so that the Chair can fully concentrate on controlling the meeting.

Agenda and other notes and documents should be laid

out on the table, preferably in advance and in easily distinguishable order. Those who enjoy the destruction of a meeting take much pleasure in the distraught shuffling of untraceable papers by the person who, in command of neither self nor meeting, should be controlling both. Try stapling coloured attachments to vital documents, especially those that are themselves small.

A lectern, table or standing model, may be useful for any speaker faced with a lengthy performance or the need to read. It makes for easier handling of notes and papers, which are brought nearer to eye level. It also helps conquer the wandering or gesticulating hand syndrome.

Desk lecterns, folding and portable or solid and firm, may be brought from specialist suppliers or built by your local handyman or tame carpenter. The table variety takes valuable space when you stand and blocks your view when you sit, and you cannot move away to the standing lectern.

Lecturers and guest speakers, though, may prefer to work from a lectern. For a large hall, the self-standing lectern should be one with built-in light and (at best) attached microphone.

If you are in the chair, organise minimum distractions from the job of chairing. If you are the speaker, the object of notes, lighting and amplification should be to leave you as free as possible to concentrate on your words.

For any other than the most important address, in which every word counts and may be held against you, it is a grave error to read your speech. Use notes.

Notes are signposts. They should set out the main ideas, briefly and clearly, so that you can see them at a swift glance. They may also include key phrases. They *must* include, written large and clear, any names to be referred to which you may forget.

Notes should be on cards. Postcard size is best. They can then be:

● Easily held in one hand . . .

● Simply shuffled, if you decide in advance to change the order of argument or presentation . . .

- Conveniently added to. Keep additional cards handy, preferably in a pocket; or subtracted from – remove the unwanted item and chuck it . . .

- Flicked aside or dropped, as the talk or speech proceeds and the subject is either covered or, in the flow of the talk, omitted . . .

- Checked – in a break in the flow – perhaps (most happily) during applause or laughter – to ensure that crucial items or arguments are not omitted.

Main errors of note users:

- Allowing others to prepare their notes. By all means get colleagues, subordinates or researchers to prepare the material, but make your own notes. You can recognise and refer to them and they can lead to any other documents from which you may wish to quote, or to which you may have to refer in order to cope with questions or interruptions . . .

- Including too much in any one note. At best, each card should bear only half a dozen words . . .

- Invisible writing – which includes typing. Cards should have few words, boldly written, with attention drawn to key items by coloured underlining . . .

- Inflexibility – or believing that notes must be followed. The great advantage of notes over scripts is – flexibility. Do not lose it. Notes are guides . . . pointers . . . aids – not crutches or stretchers. Be their master, not their slave . . .

Finally: Hold the notes firmly in one hand or leave them on lectern or table. Do not look down at or read them while you are speaking. Most amateurs habitually put their heads and eyes down to the notes. Professionals always either lift the notes up to the eye, minimising those regrettable moments of lost eye contact between speaker and audience, or look down during pauses in their word flow, at best during applause that their words have earned.

41 The Press

Sir Henry Wotton, a distinguished British diplomat of the 17th century, once defined 'an ambassador' as 'an honest man sent to lie abroad for the good of his country'. When he himself was teased about this by the newspapers, he added a postscript: 'A newswriter,' said Sir Henry, 'is a man without virtue who lies at home, for himself!'

Happily, newspapers and those who work for them will generally treat their victims with more kindness and respect than they often deserve. But meetings with the press require handling with skill.

To attract the press to your meeting, celebration or other occasion, you need a story. Create one. Have you not a famous personality to fête, a festival or an anniversary to celebrate? Tell the journalistic troops in advance, and then hope for the best. If the day is quiet, you may be lucky and the news hawks may swoop. But compete with unexpected sensation – a murder or hijacking, a political disaster or some other joyful and newsworthy event – and prepare to welcome only your most loyal of allies.

Put out a press release, before or after. But produce a story that is new ... news ... Aim it at your market and it has at least a chance. To turn out the familiar is to invite rejection.

Avoid clichés – in story or in words. The journalists'
job is to find and to print the news. If you 'clitch', as Ernest
Bevin put it, they will treat you with the yawn you deserve.

When you meet the press, they will usually do as they
are done by. Trust them and you will be trusted. Take great
care, though, to spell out what is and what is not embargoed
and until when and (especially) that which is either off the
record or non-attributable, as opposed to quotable and your
own. By following this rule with journalists, local and national, for over a quarter-century in public life, I have never
had a confidence abused by the press.

You may, of course, get misquoted – usually by human
error but occasionally by deliberation, direct or through slant-
ing or selection. Fleet Street once proclaimed that Tony Benn
recorded his speeches so that he could rehear them and work
out for the future how to improve on his applause. I asked
him: 'Is that correct?' 'Yes,' he said. 'I do record my speeches,
but not for that reason. Since I not only started doing this,
but telling the press that my machine was running, I have
found myself far less frequently misquoted!' Since then, I
have usually carried that tiny, pocket, micro-recorder. At
any meeting, public or private, of any importance at which
the press is present – and at some where I wish it had been
and want to provide an accurate report, in retrospect – my
recorder sits prominently on the table.

If the press do turn up, consider their convenience and
comfort. Where appropriate, provide a table, chair and
refreshment. But respect their integrity as you would have
them respect their own. As one mordant columnist told a
managing director who had laid on a sumptuous pre-meeting
spread for the newsman: 'You should not feed the hand that
bites you!'

Instead, choose a convenient time. About 10.30 a.m.
is good. The press are at work and their reports will catch
the evening media, as well as the next day's papers. Evenings
and weekends are generally bad, which is why some politicians with a nasty story to hide will inform the press at
about 6 p.m. on a Saturday, too late for the Sunday morning
papers and too early for the Monday editions.

Then recognise that even an energetic press person does

not look for extra work. A well-prepared and presented press kit or (at least) the agenda of the meeting with (if practicable) quotable extracts from main speeches – provide these and your prospects of cover greatly improve.

These basic rules apply whether the press are coming to your meeting or whether the meeting is specifically for the press. They apply not only to newspapers, but also to radio and TV. Give the press fair warning and treatment before, during and after the session, and you will win their appreciation and (at best) some words of approbation. Conversely: Those who spurn the press can scarcely expect fair cover.

If you consider that your treatment has been inadequate, cavalier, discourteous or unfair, then join the club! You are now a professional. Your best reaction is usually silence, otherwise you may compound the unpleasantness. Sometimes, though, the attacks are repeated and unwarranted and require protest. You could go direct to the Press Council, but do try the editor first.

Not long ago, a gossip column in a national daily saw fit to make precisely the same attack on me, in identical words, twice within a few weeks. I wrote a note to my friend, the Editor. I asked whether I had done something to offend them and, if so, perhaps they would let me know. If not, then was there any particular reason for these attacks, which would appear to be without provocation or fairness? Quoting President Truman, I recognised that if I did not like the heat, perhaps I should get out of the kitchen. Still: What was it all about?

The reply was friendly and apologetic. They appreciated my reference to the kitchen, but agreed that they should not have served so soon the same course, with the same curried insults! Since when, and hopefully on a permanent basis, that columnist has more often left me alone. To requote and misquote Groucho Marx: 'If he never writes about me again, it will be too often!'

So choose your invitees and your words with care and, if you are lucky, the press will put on the record that which you and your colleagues would want, and the rest will be forgotten.

42 Recordings and Photography

The alternative to relying entirely on memory or to taking notes at the time or making them after is to use a tape recorder. You may 'bug' your own speeches, but if you are recording anyone else's words, tell them so.

During the luncheon break at a meeting of an international organisation, security people 'swept' the room. Under the table of an East European delegation they found a carefully concealed 'bug'. The Chairman protested to the leader of the delegation. 'Why did you do that to us?' he asked.

'Oh come on,' retorted the culprit. 'You know perfectly well that we have to report back to our Government. Why not let us do so with accuracy?' Not nice.

Then there was the notorious case of the motor industry luncheon at which a guest kept a tape recorder under the table. A senior executive made a racist remark which the guest then made public. The executive was forced to resign.

It may not be nice to record other people's words. It is even less so to have your own shameful thoughts preserved for the delight of your enemies. It will be no excuse for you to say: 'It was a private occasion . . .'

A distinguished ambassador saw fit to give an 'off the record' press briefing. He was later quoted as saying that he did not consider that his Government had much chance of prolonged survival. He survived only a few weeks. His Government ran its full term! Moral: the only thoughts which are truly off the record are those kept in mind. Once moved on to the tongue, they may be recorded – at the time or after, on paper or machine or by memory.

That said: most recording is done openly. The journalist places a tape recorder on the table. Speakers at a meeting are asked to come to the microphone, so that their words can be properly recorded and transcribed.

A luncheon was given by a Parliamentary Committee for a Head of State. I was determined to remember as best I could what the man was saying. I then observed a colleague whose viewpoint differs from my own on most issues relevant to that occastion, writing notes on the back of his menu. Reckoning that sauce for the goose was also sauce for the gander and that I would prefer to be able to check on and if necessary to contradict his recollection if he went public, I followed suit. The result made vivid and excellent reading!

As I explained in the last chapter, I sometimes carry a tiny and inexpensive tape recorder. It is powerful and fits into the palm of the hand or the pocket of the shirt. It takes a microcassette from which my secretary can transcribe, so it also doubles as a dictating machine when my others are unavailable or out of action. I sometimes use it to record my own speeches. I can then counter any misquotation; create and keep a record for my own purposes or for reproduction; supply copies to those who may need or like them; or simply file the cassette, for possible future reference.

If the occasion is sufficiently important, then you may double record. The number of ways in which the non-technical mind and the clumsy finger can combine with the fallible machine to produce silence in the place of sound are manifold. Hospitals with operating theatres keep their own emergency generators. Wise organisers of major meetings arrange back-up amplification equipment, in case the main system subsides. Police officers taking notes of important events or statements do so in pairs. If you need certainty in your record of a meeting, double up your recording.

Janner's Law on Corroboration: 'Never lie alone!' In

law and in reality, a contemporaneous record of a meeting
is the best evidence of its proceedings. This can also be
done by camera.

French film-maker Jean-Luc Godard once said: 'Photo-
graphy is truth. And cinema is truth, twenty-four times a
second.' In truth, photographs are lies through a lens, and
films are to photos as statistics to figures – a multiplication
of untruths. Treat the camera with caution.

I boast a brilliant American cousin called Harold Johns
– he would have been a Janner, had my American family
not changed the name, so as to make it easier for their compat-
riots to pronounce! Anyway, Harold is a genius touch-up
artist. After watching him remove aircraft from skies,
blemishes from faces and even boys from bicycles, I have
never again believed a photograph.

In New York, I once bought a volume of Shakespeare's
collected works, in Yiddish. The fly-leaf bore the following
modest caption: 'Shakespeare – Ubergezetst und varbessert'
– 'Shakespeare – translated and improved'! What the transla-
tor did for Shakespeare, cousin Harold performs for commercial art.

You need photographs – of your meeting, yourself, your
colleagues, your business? Then commission an expert. If
his or her work needs translation or improvement, that too
may be bought at a price.

'What a beautiful child!' the election candidate gushed
to the proud mother.

'Oh, you should see his photographs!' she replied.

That should not have surprised the politician, because
every celebrity, however minor, is frequently told: 'Why, you
do look better on the box!' Make-up does marvels and so
does the camera. So how can you best use it to create and
to project your image or that of your gathering or organisation?

You must first decide what you require. Do you need
an action shot, maybe inspecting your new department, con-
gratulating an inventive employee or examining and display-
ing a newly marketed invention?

For your picture to be propelled into print at the expense
of others, it needs style, originality and must either be or
vividly illustrate – *news*. *News*papers, national or local, trade

or industry, are invariably starved of space. To win enough for your photograph needs the same eye for your journalistic market as you seek for your meeting, your product, your service or your organisation.

So pick your photographers; give them full instructions; then follow theirs. Let them set and sell the scene. Be patient and understand their problems, as they must yours.

Negotiate terms in advance. Buy the copyright, if you can, so that you can decide where, when and how to reproduce the photographs, and do not leave the negotiating fees until after the work is done.

When you receive your 'contact sheets' – rough prints or proofs – take your choice... order enlargements... or, if time is crucial, leave it to your expert to make the decisions. That includes, where appropriate, giving the final effort the Harold Johns treatment.

What, then, about getting onto other people's photographs? How do you capture the centre of the recorded stage?

Start by being there at the beginning. Press photographers have a disconcerting habit of arriving at meetings either early or late. If you are late, you may be sure that the camera will have been and gone – 'deadline to meet, sorry...' or 'He had another assignment to get to...' or (in truth) maybe he simply wanted to get home to soothe his wife or to play with his children.

Of course, if you arrive on time, you may reasonably expect the photographer to be late. 'Sorry... I had to deal with another assignment... meet another deadline...' Or, simply: 'I was given the wrong instructions...' So put your time at the camera's disposal and hope for the best.

Then think about how you wish your image to appear. Dress and behave accordingly.

Labour leader Michael Foot suffered election catastrophe, nurtured by film and photograph showing him dressed in a way that the electorate considered unsuitable for a Prime Minister – at its worst, in casual clothes at the Cenotaph for the Remembrance Parade. Neil Kinnock does not make the same mistake.

Adjust your dress and your demeanour to suit the occasion. It is worse to be trapped into photographed laughter at a funeral – personal or commercial – than frowning at the announcement of a supposed company joy.

Relax your face and body, so as to appear natural. The stilted, Victorian pose may be fine for the family album, but not as the projection of the modern executive. Do not relax your mind or lose your concentration in the presence of the almighty camera, or you have only yourself to blame if those who would do you harm use your photograph as their weapon.

43 Pastimes

Are you in town – or in Britain – for a meeting, a conference, a seminar, an organisational gathering? Then boredom threatens! So consider: How can you best and most speedily pass those hours whilst others are passing or rejecting resolutions or motions? How can you properly and invisibly entertain your own mind whilst others insist upon expressing theirs?

Here, then, are Dr Janner's recipes for the mental ailments of meeting-mongers, culled from over thirty years of personal suffering. The extent to which you will need them will depend upon your own threshold of pain.

In Charles Dickens' *A Tale of Two Cities*, the amazing Madame Defarge found it necessary to concentrate on her knitting as the victims of the guillotine passed by in the Revolutionary tumbrils and as their heads dropped bleeding into baskets.

How often have you observed the destruction of a good case by a bad speaker . . . the ruin of a splendid day, when you could have been enjoying the sights or happy company or even burrowing into your workload, while instead you are pinned by courtesy, custom or convention or because you must listen to others who will in due corse (and when will that be?) hearken unto you?

Anyway: Here are some of my favourite escape mechanisms.

First: If you yourself will or may wish to participate,

plan your words, your speech, your attack, your question. Jot down: The objects of your exercise, the purpose of your operation . . . the strength of your case and the weakness of its opposition.

As speeches drone on, put your points onto separate cards. Always bring some with you to a meeting, for notes to yourself and to pass to others . . . Inscribe the points made by proponents and allies, noting how these could and should be better put . . . and by opponents and enemies, and how these could and should be best demolished.

Next: Listen to what the speaker is saying and then work out what the words really mean. On the principle that you should not only know your enemies but choose them – with the proviso that you should never make an unnecessary enemy – do you want this person on your side? Is the speaker who speaks on your side best suited to be on the other? If he or she is already on the other, then what words, campaign or approach by you or by whom else could shift the balance in your worthy direction?

A newly elected Tory MP at his first Question Time said to his veteran neighbour: 'Well, here we are. The Government is up front on this side; and the enemy is over there on the other.'

'Sorry, chum,' came the answer. 'You've got it wrong. Here we are . . . the Government is up front – and the Opposition is on the other side. The enemy,' he added, with a sweep of his arm at his own colleagues, 'the enemy is all around us!'

Most MPs have most of their friends on their own side of the House, but many have many on the other. Too many of our most dangerous opponents sit around us, on our own side of the room, hall or chamber. As Wellington remarked when reviewing a contingent of troops sent to him in Spain: 'I don't know what effect these men will have upon the enemy, but, by God, they terrify me!' So, as a sensible diversion, why not list those on your side who are against you?

Next: Take three separate sheets of paper and list the following:

● Errors in presentation . . . what the speaker is doing

wrong . . . how the presentation to which you have been sentenced could be increased in impact and reduced in length.

● Clichés. In the days of the Bible, there was already 'nothing new under the sun'. But the English language, like most others, is blessed with a rainbow of imagery. If I can teach the law on data protection and keep my audience attentive and amused for five solid hours then surely your speaker could have expunged the cliché and replaced it with a flare of wit or wisdom – if not his own, then at least borrowed or quoted from someone else? Note each failure.

● Conversely – and for this you will in almost every case require a much smaller sheet – note quotable remarks, jokes, witticisms – plus ideas of style or content worth copying.

   Historian A.L. Rowse was asked in a TV interview: 'How do you write your books?'

   He replied: 'I don't really. I keep a notebook as I go along and they almost write themselves.'

   Maybe *your* meeting notes could form the basis of a collection, a guide, an article or a book for others to read? If not, they will certainly help you to imitate the words or ways of others who succeed and to avoid their most awful clichés of expression or of presentation.

Next: Write your letters – on paper provided. The back of an agenda sheet or any part of the dinner menu will serve nicely. Or get your revenge on the speaker by using his supplied biography.

If the speaker sees you writing, he or she will be flattered. There is an immediate presumption that you are noting vital points.

When one orator arrived home after a meeting, his wife asked him: 'Well, Fred, how did it go?'

'Tremendous,' he said. 'The press were so interested that they put down their pencils and listened!'

The converse is more likely and much easier to get away

with: The speaker observes that you were so impressed with
the diet that you could not put down your knife and fork.

Next: When did you last check your diary and your
engagements . . . your accounts and your prospects . . . or your
future plans, for this journey or visit, this day or occasion
or conference – or for the next? Lay your diary, notebook,
accounts sheet or what-have-you-with-you inside the file or
folder or pad provided. Keep your pen or pencil in your
hand, so that you can apparently be taking notes . . . look
up frequently at the speaker . . . and get on with your own
affairs.

With only a little practice, you will learn to keep your
gaze on the speaker with apparent rapt attention, while your
mind is intent on anything else of greater interest.

William Wordsworth wrote about a field of daffodils:

When oft upon my couch I lie,
In vacant or in pensive mood,
That flash upon that inward eye
That is the bliss of solitude.

The best exercise for the victim of meetings is to practise
looking with the outer eye at the speaker while training the
inward eye to achieve solitude in that loneliness which is
a crowd.

Conversely: Never close your eyes, even to concentrate.
You will not be forgiven for the discourtesy of apparent
slumber.

The late Lord Salisbury is reputed to have dreamed
that he was speaking in the House of Lords. He woke up
and found that he was! Too many of us dream at meetings
that we are somewhere else and wake up and find that we
are not.

It is the waking dream that needs cultivation. Doodle . . .
play noughts and crosses, boxes or any other game with yourself or with your neighbour . . . count the squares in the ceiling
or the size of male or female content of the audience . . .
or like Madame Defarge, knit while the heads roll and the
speakers bore. But for passing meeting time with most benefit
and speed, nothing beats your own thoughts, masked by the
glazed gaze of apparent attention. Nothing, that is, except

spotting the dull meeting in advance and keeping the maximum distance away from it that courtesy, other engagements or feigned illness – or the requirements or ailments of your spouse or friend – can achieve.

44 In Conclusion

There is an art to the end of a meeting. General de Gaulle once described life as 'a great voyage, ending in shipwreck'. If your meeting is to land safely, then the end must be planned from the start. So ask – yourself and colleagues:

- What is the purpose of your exercise?

- How will you know when you have achieved that purpose?

- What should you then do to bring the meeting to an appropriate end?

- What is the action which must then be taken – and by whom – and will each know what is expected of him or of her?

- How can you best ensure that the meeting ends in the right mood?

Far too many participants leave most meetings saying to themselves or to others: 'What a waste of time that was!' They return for more meetings for a variety of motives:

- The wish to attend is greater than the urge to keep away...

- Their attendance is required – either by superiors or by the need to become superior . . .
- Their attendance is expected – either because it is needed or because 'noblesse oblige' . . .
- To dispel boredom or loneliness . . .
- In the hope of acquiring information or, more likely, with the intention of providing it . . .
- Or, hopefully, to take part in a constructive discussion . . . to propagate ideas or ideals . . . or even to learn . . .

Before your meeting begins, consider – who is coming and why and how can you best make each feel by the end of the session that the time was well spent?

Try making checklists and marking them before you close your meeting. List One – your objectives. List Two – your participants. In a smaller meeting: has each spoken . . . been asked for a view . . . played some role? In a larger event: Have you remembered to call on everyone entitled to speak . . .?

List the topics. Has each been fairly covered, so as to give a reasonable hearing to each viewpoint?

Unfortunately, as Robert Burns remarked: 'The best laid schemes o' mice an' men gang aft a-gley'. You may plan your meeting to perfection but by its end you may not have achieved your objects or its purpose. Time is the enemy, plus length of wind.

However late the hour, though, allow a brief pause to check those lists, at best on paper but otherwise by mental agility. You may then avoid both ill-will and those fatal words, when the meeting is closed 'I'm so sorry, ladies and gentlemen . . . Can I have your attention for just another moment . . . I forgot to mention that . . . We cannot leave without looking at . . .'

'Nothing in his life,' as Malcolm says of the thane of Cawdor, 'became him like the leaving it.' You do not want the same said about your meeting.

When all is done, you rap your gavel. 'Thank you. The meeting is closed.'

Farewell, now . . . and good luck!

Index